Industrialism:
The American Experience

Inquiries into American History

Our Colonial Heritage: Plymouth and Jamestown
by William Gee White

The Middle Colonies: New York, New Jersey, Pennsylvania
by James I. Clark

The American Revolution
by D. Duane Cummins and William Gee White

The Federal Period: 1790–1800
by Lloyd K. Musselman

Andrew Jackson's America
by Thomas Koberna and Stanley Garfinkel

The American Frontier
by D. Duane Cummins and William Gee White

The Origins of the Civil War
by D. Duane Cummins and William Gee White

Reconstruction: 1865–1877
by James I. Clark

Industrialism: The American Experience
by James E. Bruner, Jr.

American Foreign Policy: 1789–1980
by Thomas A. Fitzgerald, Jr.

Contrasting Decades: The 1920's and 1930's
by D. Duane Cummins and William Gee White

Combat and Consensus: The 1940's and 1950's
by D. Duane Cummins and William Gee White

Conflict and Compromise: The 1960's and 1970's
by D. Duane Cummins

America at War: World War I and World War II
by Douglas Waitley

America at War: Korea and Vietnam
by Douglas Waitley

Women in American History
by William Jay Jacobs

Industrialism: The American Experience

James E. Bruner, Jr.

Glencoe Publishing Co., Inc.
Encino, California

Contributing Editor:

Dr. James I. Clark

REVISED EDITION

Glencoe Publishing Co., Inc.
17337 Ventura Boulevard
Encino, California 91316

Collier Macmillan Canada, Ltd.

Library of Congress Catalog Card Number: 78–187533

Printed in the United States of America

ISBN 0-02-652820-7

1 2 3 4 5 82 81 80 79

To my grandparents,
GUY WALTER and ANNA MAY JEFFERIES,
whose admiration for Eugene V. Debs
inspired me to study American history.

CONTENTS

The Brooklyn Bridge—a triumph of the new technology—was completed in 1883.

Library of Congress

INTRODUCTION

In 1830 Americans had scarcely pushed their frontier across the Mississippi River. Sixty years later settlement was so widespread that the Bureau of the Census could declare that a frontier no longer existed. During those six decades, Americans had populated a continent. They had also created an industrial nation.

About twelve million people lived in the United States in 1830. New York, the largest city, held 200,000; Chicago, a muddy little village on the shores of Lake Michigan, had hardly begun. In 1890, the nation's population reached sixty-three million. New York had grown to three million people and Chicago contained slightly more than one million. The natural increase in population had been greatly augmented by the influx of millions of immigrants from Europe and Asia.

Long-distance travel within the nation in 1830 was for the most part limited to horses or horse-drawn vehicles and to sail-driven boats on rivers, lakes, and a few hundred miles of canals. There were only about thirty miles of railroad in the entire country. By 1890, the nation had been crisscrossed by 167,000 miles of track, and steamboats plied not only the Great Lakes but the Ohio and Mississippi rivers as well.

There was hardly any steel production in 1830. In 1870 it amounted to only 37,500 tons; at that time, Britain, the world's leader, produced 225,000 tons. Before the end of the century the positions had been dramatically reversed—the United States, thirteen million tons, Great Britain, five million. To cite the growth of another industry, in 1830 the total value of cotton manufactures was under $45 million; it had surpassed $115 million by 1860.

The Gross National Product, a unit of economic measurement equal to the total value of all goods and services produced, is a twentieth-century invention. But it is estimated that the GNP in 1870 was about $6 billion and by 1890 double that amount.

In 1830, farmers plowed their fields behind horses or oxen, and sometimes got into harness themselves; they sowed and reaped by hand. By 1890, horse-drawn drills, cultivators, and reapers as well as steam-driven threshing machines were common.

Early in the nineteenth century the rate at which a man could travel determined the speed of communication, and people had only candles and oil lamps to drive away the darkness. By 1890 the telegraph had long since ceased to be a novelty and many city dwellers had telephones. During the 1890's electric lighting rapidly replaced gas and oil illumination in the cities.

In 1830 trade and commerce offered the principal avenue to great wealth. By 1890 there were numerous ways to make a fortune—in steel, oil, railroads, meat-packing, mail-order selling, and in many other endeavors. And some of the fortunes were truly huge. In one year Andrew Carnegie's steel company made $40 million in profits. As principal owner, Carnegie took $25 million of that. Carnegie sold his company in 1901 for $491 million. His share was $225 million. Carnegie's income was enormous, but that of many other men was nearly as awe-inspiring. And at that time there were no income taxes, corporate or personal.

In the opinion of many people, Andrew Carnegie, John D. Rockefeller, Philip Armour, and other captains of industry richly deserved their wealth. It was their just reward for their entrepreneurial risks, their business acumen, and the benefits of jobs and products they bestowed upon the country. To others they were, as President Theodore Roosevelt later characterized them, simply malefactors of great wealth.

The industrialization of America produced thousands of new products and services, a higher standard of living for many, and great wealth for a few. It also placed control of capital and production in the hands of a few men, pro-

Library of Congress

East Fifth Street, New York City, in 1890. Paved streets were uncommon in poor districts, and municipal services like garbage collection were almost unknown.

duced monopolies in railroad and other services, created dreadful slums in the large cities, and, in the opinion of some people, erected a rigid class structure with a downtrodden proletariat at the bottom. Industrial workers' wages ranged between $400 and $500 a year for an average sixty-hour work week. Roughly 285,000 children between the ages of ten and fifteen were employed in factories. Industrial accidents were common; there was no workmen's compensation, health insurance, or sick leave, to say nothing of company retirement or social security benefits. Government intervention on the side of employers, blacklists, lockouts, and strong-armed strikebreaking methods helped keep unions weak. By 1900, the total union membership in the nation was 868,500—about four percent of the total workers in industry and transportation. One guess placed the number of people living in poverty—undernourished, underclothed, and poorly housed—at ten million; of these, probably four million were public paupers, dependent on public or private charity. Workers and paupers were especially bad off during depressions, two of which—in the 1870's and 1890's—were severe.

Farmers also suffered from the workings of a market that often mystified them. Prices for wheat, for example, were set in the cities and, thanks to international trade, were influenced by worldwide production. To get their crops to market, farmers had to rely on railroads that charged pretty much what they pleased. Individual farmers in most instances had only one railroad to choose from. Farmers were fierce competitors—with each other—but they were helpless to compete as a group in a market influenced or rigged by forces over which they had no control.

Industrialization developed with little government regulation but with much government help. Until 1860, owing partly to southern influence in Washington, there was relatively little federal government spending for internal improvements. Tariffs usually were imposed only to provide the government with revenue and were generally low. The picture changed after Republicans won control of the federal government in 1860—and they maintained this control until 1912, with the exception of two conservative Democratic administrations in the late 1880's and early 1890's. High protective tariffs became common in the 1890's, huge land grants were made to railroad companies, and homestead laws encouraging settlement in the West were enacted. The homestead laws frequently benefited land speculators and the railroads more than the settlers, who sometimes found themselves on waterless acreage unsuited to the plow. Government—state and national—became primarily an instrument of business and industrial interests. Regulation and unionization were discouraged, bribery and corruption to obtain favorable legislation and lucrative government contracts were not uncommon, and in the 1890's the United States Senate became known as a rich man's club.

Toward the end of the century, criticism of the state of America's industrialized and urbanized society grew louder. A measure of political democracy had been achieved early in the 1800's when the states abolished property restrictions on voting; by 1870, all male citizens over the age of twenty-one, whatever their color or economic status, were legally entitled to vote. But political democracy did not prevent glaring and acute economic and social inequalities from developing. In the late nineteenth century, some reformers feared that if steps were not taken to eliminate some of the worst inequities, revolutionary upheaval would be the result. They advocated, among other things, regulation of railroads and other businesses, legislation favorable to unionization, an end to trusts and monopolies, well-enforced compulsory education laws that would ensure at least elementary schooling for all, increased taxes on business and industry, an end to child labor, government regulation of hours and other working conditions for women, clean government, and the abolition of slums. All of this, they felt, required state and national government intervention on the side of the common people. Few reformers denied that competition was an important and on the whole salutary part of economic and social life. They wished, however, to abolish competition which degraded human dignity and human worth. Few except socialists condemned the whole capitalist system. Reformers generally accepted its economic and philosophical premises, and wanted only to eliminate its obvious abuses.

This book deals first with defenders and critics of the industrial *status quo* in the 1890's. It then goes on to discuss some of the great nineteenth-century industrialists, and some of the effects industrialization had on the quality of American life, especially in the cities. Finally, the book sketches progressive legislation enacted in an effort to curb abuses and eliminate inequality.

The New York Public Library

This 1885 cartoon ridicules the efforts of Henry Ward Beecher, the old abolitionist, to reconcile the theory of evolution with a belief in God the creator. When men like Herbert Spencer and William Graham Sumner applied evolutionary theory to human society and economics, many social reformers found it necessary to try to bridge the gap between the notion of "survival of the fittest" and the traditional Christian ideals of charity and ethical conduct.

INDUSTRIAL SOCIETY PRO AND CON

Two Englishmen furnished philosophical and theoretical underpinning for nineteenth-century American business and industry. One was Adam Smith, the other Charles Darwin.

Adam Smith

Adam Smith, who died in 1790, was a well-educated Scotsman and a professor of logic and moral philosophy at the University of Glasgow. In 1776, after ten years of effort, he published *The Wealth of Nations*, a monumental work in political economy. In *The Wealth of Nations*, Smith took issue with the mercantilist economic policies in vogue at the time. On the whole, mercantilism was protectionist and nationalistic. It upheld private and public monopolies, protective duties on imports that might compete with home products, and favorable trade balances—an excess of exports over imports. Mercantilists looked upon colonies as sources of raw materials and as markets, not as self-sustaining political entities. Of the three factors of production, mercantilists viewed land and capital as much more important than labor as contributors to a nation's wealth.

Smith considered labor the most important factor of production and self-interest the prime motivation for human behavior. Individuals, he argued, know best what is good for them; no one would behave contrary to his own self-interest. To further his self-interest, a person would produce goods people wanted because this would insure him the largest profit. For the same reasons of self-interest, men would work where they received the highest wages. The marketplace—the arena in which buying and selling of goods took place—indicated where people's best interest lay, and thus the marketplace was the mechanism that controlled the economy. The marketplace automatically determined price and attended to supply and demand; it was the point where everyone's self-interest was worked out to the enhancement of the public good. With the marketplace as the regulating factor, according to Smith, there would be no need for monopolies, government control or aid, or protective tariffs. Smith advocated a *laissez-faire*—literally, "allow them to do"—economy, a free economy governed only by the natural laws operating in the marketplace.

In a laissez-faire economy, if the price of labor was to be controlled by the market, then it was a commodity like anything else. An employer, to serve his self-interest, would try to hire as cheaply as possible. A laborer, to serve his, would attempt to get the highest wages he could. The price arrived at would be subject to the natural law of supply and demand. Unionization, a form of monopoly, tended to circumvent this law and to interfere with the free operation of the market. A laborer was free to move to wherever he could obtain high wages; it served his self-interest to do so. The idea of a "living wage" was, of course, foreign to Smith's marketplace and to his labor-as-a-commodity concepts. The worker was dependent upon the wage he could demand as an individual in the marketplace. If this wage was below a level on which he could live, it was merely unfortunate and no one's fault, especially not the fault of the employer, who was also subject to the laws of the market.

Economic thinking in the nineteenth century demanded some standard of monetary value on which everyone agreed. Gold served this purpose. It was both a circulating medium and a reserve against which currency was issued and for which currency could be exchanged upon demand. The amount of gold reserves on hand placed a ceiling on the quantity of currency available; currency could not therefore be increased just by printing more of it. Gold was also an international medium of exchange, used to settle trade accounts between nations.

Like all practical men, American businessmen and industrialists picked and chose among economic theories as it suited their purposes. The laissez-faire commodity theory of labor was acceptable. So was the idea of nonregulating government. Protective tariffs were another matter; manufacturers tended to favor them. Businessmen and industrialists also tended to favor other kinds of government help, such as land grants to railroads and court decisions that found labor unions to be conspiracies in restraint of trade and therefore illegal. Insofar as adherence to Adam Smith's principles did not harm or endanger business interests, the nineteenth was a laissez-faire century.

Charles Darwin

Charles Darwin was a naturalist. After a four-year voyage around the world, during which he made detailed observations of flora and fauna and collected thousands of specimens, Darwin began to develop a radically new theory of the relationship of organisms to their environment. He published this theory in 1859 in *The Origin of Species.* Species, Darwin concluded, had not been created. They had evolved over thousands—in some cases, millions—of years. Some, owing to an inability to adapt to environmental changes, became extinct. Others, able to change as the environment gradually altered, survived. Those that did survive were selected naturally, that is, by the interaction of organism and environment. Competition for survival was keen and only the fittest—although not necessarily the strongest physically—succeeded.

Brown Brothers

Charles Darwin.

Some Englishmen and Americans made Darwin's theory of evolution into a theory to explain society and economics. Although Darwin had been concerned with explaining the successful development of species or whole populations, successful nineteenth-century Americans were concerned with explaining why some individuals within the same species got to the top of the heap while others failed. "The struggle for existence" and "survival of the fittest" became catch phrases. These phrases suggested a society that resembled a blood-stained jungle in which the strong devoured the weak, which was not at all what Darwin had been talking about. To those who espoused this view, the fact that some men were wealthy and powerful while many others were not was the best evidence of all that the fittest not only survived, but prospered as well. The free enterprise system, as they conceived it, gave everyone an equal chance for survival and riches. A person had only to labor within the system, work hard, and use his intelligence. The people who agreed with all this have been called Social Darwinists. They tended to be conservative—socially, economically, and politically. According to Richard Hofstadter,

> Darwinism was used to buttress the conservative outlook in two ways. The most popular catchwords of Darwinism, "struggle for existence" and "survival of the fittest," when applied to the life of man in society, suggested that nature would provide that the best competitors in a competitive situation would win, and that this process would lead to continuing improvement. In itself this was not a new idea, as economists could have pointed out, but it did give the force of a natural law to the idea of competitive struggle. Secondly, the idea of development over aeons brought new force to another familiar idea in conservative political theory, the conception that all sound development must be slow and unhurried.[1]

William Graham Sumner

The most influential Social Darwinist in England was Herbert Spencer; the most influential in America was William Graham Sumner. The son of a workman on the Hartford and New Haven Railroad, Sumner was educated in the public schools of Hartford, Connecticut, and in 1859 entered Yale University, where he earned a reputation as a reserved and sober-minded scholar. Ambitious to enter the ministry, he completed his theological training in Europe and in 1870 became rector of the Church of the

[1] Richard Hofstadter, *Social Darwinism in American Thought* (Boston: Beacon Press, 1965), pp. 6–7.

Redeemer in Morristown, New Jersey. Sumner's interest in social and economic questions proved greater than his devotion to religion, however, and two years later he accepted a teaching position in political and social science at Yale. There he spent the remainder of his life.

Sumner upheld the business ethic, laissez-faire capitalism, and free enterprise. Just as inexorable natural laws governed the working of the universe, he believed, so did natural laws determine man's social and economic behavior. To attempt to change or ameliorate these forces was folly. Speaking of industrial organization in his essay "The Absurd Effort to Make the World Over," Sumner said,

> The stage of the industrial organization existing at any time, and the rate of its development, are the absolutely controlling social facts. . . . It controls us all because we are in it. It creates the conditions of our existence, sets the limits of our social activity, regulates the bonds of our social relations, determines our conceptions of good and evil, suggests our life-philosophy, molds our inherited political institutions, and reforms the oldest and toughest customs, like marriage and property.[2]

In Sumner's opinion man had little control over his environment; he could do nothing about the forces that were at work in society. Man, said Sumner, "is in the stream and is swept along with it. All his sciences and philosophy come to him out of it. Therefore the tide will not be changed by us."[3] In the final analysis, according to Sumner, even government was powerless to alter social and economic forces and their effects. Government interference, to him, was not only futile but harmful as well. It only increased governmental weight on the individual citizen and eroded personal liberty. "Against this view," Sumner wrote, "nothing has ever yet been brought forward but the pure assumption which has all experience against it, that, if the state should not do things they would not be done at all. . . ."

[2] Albert Galloway Keller and Maurice R. Davie, eds., *Essays of William Graham Sumner* (New Haven, Conn.: Yale University Press, 1934), p. 93.

[3] Ibid., p. 105.

> When we are told that the state would do all things better, if we would give it more things to do, the answer is that there is nothing which the state has not tried to do, and that it has only exceptionally performed anything well, even war or royal marriages, and that, on the contrary, here in the United States, where the other policy [of noninterference by the state] has had more trial than anywhere else—favored, it is true, by circumstances—it has proved beneficent in the extreme. Therefore, if, after all, it is only a question of whether to put faith in the state or to put faith in liberty, an educated American ought not to hesitate long which to do.[4]

It was true that under unbridled capitalism a few men gained great wealth. But this too was only natural, as was the development of trusts and monopolies that furthered the accumulation of personal wealth. Individual industrialists deserved to be rich—this was their reward for the progress their efforts brought. Said Sumner,

> The captains of industry and the capitalist . . . if they are successful, win . . . great fortunes in a short time. There are no earnings which are more legitimate or for which greater services are rendered to the whole industrial body. The popular notions about this . . . assume that all the wealth accumulated by these . . . persons would be . . . just the same if they had not existed. They are supposed to have appropriated it out of the common stock. This is so far from being true that, on the contrary, their own wealth would not be but for themselves; and besides that, millions more . . . scattered in the hands of thousands, would not exist but for them.[5]

Millions of men were poor, Sumner admitted, but this was more their fault than the system's. Poverty could be eliminated, but not through government action or through the efforts of social workers and reformers:

> Let every man be sober, industrious, prudent and wise,

[4] Albert Galloway Keller, ed., *Earth-Hunger and Other Essays by William Graham Sumner* (New Haven, Conn.: Yale University Press, 1913), pp. 304–305.

[5] Keller and Davie, *Essays*, p. 97.

and bring up his children to be so likewise, and poverty will be abolished in a few generations. If it is answered that men with the best intention, cannot fulfill this precept, because they make innocent mistakes, and fall into errors in judgment, then the demand is changed, and we are now asked for a means of abolishing human error. If it be objected, again, that sober, industrious, and prudent men meet with misfortune, then the demand is for a means of abolishing misfortune.[6]

About the poor, Sumner was exceedingly tough-minded. Society had to care for true paupers and the physically incapacitated. That was above question. But it was not those groups that social reformers became excited about, it seemed to Sumner.

I do not wish to be understood now as saying that nothing ought to be done for these people by those who are stronger and wiser. That is not my point. What I want to do is to point out the thing which is overlooked and the error which is made in all these charitable efforts. The notion is accepted as if it were not open to question that if you help the inefficient and vicious you may gain something for society or you may not, but that you lose nothing. This is a complete mistake. Whatever capital you divert to the support of a shiftless and good-for-nothing person is so much diverted from some other employment, and that means from somebody else. . . . Capital is force. If it goes one way it cannot go another. . . .[7]

Sentiment—social reformers' stock-in-trade, Sumner believed—was irrelevant to the problem. According to Sumner,

We can find no sentiment whatever in nature; that all comes from man. We can find no disposition at all in nature to conform her operations to man's standards, so as to do what is pleasant or advantageous to man rather than anything else. Before the tribunal of nature a man has no more right to life than a rattlesnake; he has no more right to

[6] Ibid., p. 109.
[7] Ibid., p. 477.

> liberty than any wild beast; his right to the pursuit of happiness is nothing but a license to maintain the struggle for existence if he can find within himself the powers with which to do it.[8]

According to Sumner, when social reformers focused on the indigent and the seemingly unfortunate, they made a terrible mistake: they overlooked that bulwark of society, "the Forgotten Man." Sumner offered the following definition of "the Forgotten Man":

> He is the simple, honest laborer, ready to earn his living by productive work. We pass him by because he is independent, self-supporting, and asks no favors. He does not appeal to the emotions or excite the sentiments. He only wants to make a contract and fulfill it, with respect on both sides and favor on neither side. He must get his living out of the capital of the country. The larger the capital, which is wasted on the vicious, the idle, and the shiftless, is so much taken from the capital available to reward the independent and productive laborer. But we stand with our backs to the independent and productive laborer all the time. We do not remember him because he makes no clamor; but I appeal to you whether he is not the man who ought to be remembered first of all, and whether, on any sound social theory, we ought not to protect him against the burdens of the good-for-nothing.[9]

Sumner had a suggestion for his readers concerning charity:

> The silly notion is that the beggars live at the expense of the rich, but the truth is that those who eat and produce not, live at the expense of those who labor and produce. The next time that you are tempted to subscribe a dollar to a charity, I do not tell you not to do it, because after you have fairly considered the matter, you may think it right to do it, but I do ask you to stop and remember the Forgotten Man and understand that if you put your dollar in the savings bank it will go to swell the capital of the

[8] Ibid., p. 385.
[9] Ibid., p. 485.

The New York Public Library

During the depression of 1873, a number of private charitable organizations set up "soup-houses" to feed the poor.

> country which is available for division amongst those who, while they earn it, will reproduce it with increase.[10]

Besides, said Sumner, trying to help the people reformers regarded as unfortunate and downtrodden was futile social meddling. It was an endless, thankless task, for those people did not really want to be helped.

> The people in the slums and tenement houses will not give up the enjoyment of the streets for any amount of rural comfort. Other classes try to help them, assuming that, to them, crowds, noise, filth, contagious diseases, and narrow quarters, must be painful. The evidence is that they like the life, and are indifferent to what others consider its evils and discomforts. They like it because it satisfies the strongest desires in the mores of our time. The people in the slums feel the same desires as those other people who have clubs, balls, visitors, the park, opera, theater, and all the other means of excitement, gossip, and entertainment which make up fashionable city life.[11]

[10] Ibid., p. 478.
[11] Ibid., p. 93.

William Graham Sumner was no more tender-minded about vice and crime:

> Vice is its own curse. If we let nature alone, she cures vice by the most frightful penalties . . . a drunkard in the gutter is just where he ought to be. Nature is working away at him to get him out of the way. . . . Nine-tenths of our measures for preventing vice are really protective towards it because they ward off the penalty.[12]

Attempts to reform criminals were worse than folly. Such efforts were downright harmful to society:

> A criminal is a man who, instead of working with and for society, turns his efforts against the common welfare in some way or other. He disturbs order, violates harmony, invades the security and happiness of others, wastes and destroys capital. If he is put to death, it is on the ground that he has forfeited all right to existence in society by the magnitude of his offenses against its welfare. If he is imprisoned, it is simply a judgment of society upon him that he is so mischievous to the society that he must be segregated from it. His punishment is a warning to him to reform himself, just exactly like the penalties inflicted by God and nature on vice. A man who has committed crime is, therefore, a burden on society and an injury to it. He is destructive and not a productive force and everybody is worse off for his existence than if he did not exist. Whence, then, does he obtain a right to be taught or reformed at the public expense?[13]

Capitalists and captains of industry applauded Sumner. He made what they were doing seem right, in accord with the natural order of things. But his consistency sometimes dismayed them. He was against *all* government interference, and that included high protective tariffs, a form of government subsidy much favored by industrialists of the time. Sumner was also anti-imperialistic, not a popular attitude at the time of the Spanish-American War and the acquisition of American colonies. His opposition to the

[12] Ibid., p. 481.
[13] Ibid., p. 485.

Spanish-American War caused many industrialists to demand his dismissal from Yale. In general, Sumner regarded war and preparation for war a waste of valuable resources.

Lester Frank Ward

William Graham Sumner stood on a mountaintop proclaiming his hard-headed Social Darwinism and pleading that natural laws of human behavior be allowed to work unfettered. On another peak stood sociologist Lester Frank Ward, offering the nation a different point of view.

Ward's interests, broad and varied, included biology, anthropology, psychology, and geology as well as sociology. In the 1880's and 1890's he worked as both a geologist and a paleontologist for the United States Geological Survey. Author of several articles on the natural sciences, he became best known for his leadership in American sociology.

Lester Frank Ward was a high priest of the scientific method as a means to solve social problems. In his devotion to science he went so far as to say:

> We can scarcely fix our mind upon one temporal blessing that we enjoy to-day, from the luxury of good food to the luxury of good health for which we are not indebted to science. But besides these countless physical blessings, science affords the highest and purest intellectual delight. It has let us into the arena of the infinite universe, and taught us to contemplate the wonders of nature, from the vast firmament of revolving spheres to the infinitesimal world of moving atoms; from the sparkling crystal to the living organism, the contemplation of which sublime truths yields to the mind a holier ecstasy than any reflections upon the character and attributes of anthropomorphic deities, or any selfish hopes of a future eternity of bliss. And when we remember that which is the crowning glory of science, that with all these blessings she has never cost one human life, one drop of human blood, one pang of human suffering, how long will the world hesitate to pronounce its decision?[14]

[14] Lester Frank Ward, *Glimpses of the Cosmos*, 4 vols. (New York: G. P. Putnam's Sons, 1913), 1: 55.

Man's intelligence, said Ward, placed him at the top of the evolutionary scale. Because he had intelligence man could plan and order his world as he saw fit. No longer did he need to bend to natural laws and play the deadly game of survival of the fittest. To interfere, to regulate, to plan and deliberately change were simply intelligent things to do. And the means by which to bring about a better world was the most intelligent ever devised—the scientific method. Groups of men—and governments—as well as individuals could use it.

Unlike Sumner, Ward was far from cheerful about the concentration of wealth in the hands of a few men. He considered wealth not an absolute possession but a trust for the benefit of society, a means by which a person could acquire leisure time that could be used to gain knowledge and provide social benefits. Ward thought that American industrial captains had not fulfilled their responsibilities.

> The so-called men of leisure, who have accomplished these great results, have really been the most industrious of all men. Leisure, in this sense, merely means relief from the necessity of performing statical work in order to be able to perform dynamic work. . . . But how few understand it in this sense! The vulgar notion of leisure, secured by ample means, is immunity from all work. Many such people give freely to the poor, found asylums and endow colleges, and believe that, with this, they have executed their trust. This is a wholly false view. The wealthy have a higher duty to perform. They are under obligations directly to themselves and indirectly to society. Wealth alone does not make true manhood. . . . Culture alone can make these possessions real. Industry alone can make them count as social factors. The heirs of wealth, the legatees of rank and noble blood, the children of great men, and the descendants of geniuses, are too apt to imagine that nothing is left for them to do. No greater mistake could be made, and none leads more directly to degeneracy. In this age all value is measured by labor, and this is not more true of matter than it is of mind, of material than of mental wealth. What makes one man superior to another is superior acquire-

ment; at least, so far is this the case that the greatest natural superiority, without acquirement, counts for nothing in the world of thought.[15]

Ward foresaw an obvious danger in the accumulation of wealth unaccompanied by a feeling of social responsibility:

> Great revolutions are often caused by persistence in old habits in defiance of a changed public sentiment, and they might in most cases be prevented by a wise recognition of this change and a gradual conforming to its demands. The people are frequently forced into open revolt by an obstinate refusal to do this on the part of those holding power of whatever kind. Most past revolutions have been political, and aimed at liberation from some form of despotism. The revolutions of the future are likely to be social, not directed against the State, but against a power higher than the State—the power of wealth—producing great monopolies and sustaining a large non-producing and idle class, or caste, sheltered behind the forms of law, but odious to the changing spirit of the age.[16]

Speaking of Sumner's doctrine of noninterference with natural laws, Ward said,

> The author [Sumner] inveighs . . . against meddling with natural laws, and interfering with the natural flow of events. He seems never to have reflected that practical art as the product of applied science, and which alone constitutes man a civilized being, is the exclusive effect of his meddling and interfering with the natural course of physical phenomena. The inventor is just the "meddler" he is belaboring.[17]

According to Ward, Sumner's laissez-faire doctrine, if carried to its logical conclusion, would be suicidal.

And the prime "meddler," as far as Ward was concerned, could well be government. There was nothing inherently inefficient in government-operated enterprises; in fact, they

[15] Ibid., 3: 50.
[16] Ibid., pp. 53–54.
[17] Ibid., p. 304.

could be superior in efficiency to privately operated endeavors. As Ward pointed out with apparent relish:

> We now see there, in the land of Adam Smith [Great Britain], regulation of railroads, state education, postal telegraphy, the parcels-post law, temperance laws, landlord and tenant laws, an Irish land act, and a great body of legislation arising in large part from what is popularly called the "national conscience." In general, foreign commerce is there left free, as is obviously the true policy for an almost exclusively commercial nation; but when it is wished to discourage the importation of luxuries or injurious commodities, such as distilled liquors, the duties are unsparingly laid on, often amounting to prohibition.
>
> In America, to secure national self-dependence, develop mineral and other resources, encourage inventive talent and home manufacturers, diversify population, and avoid redundant transportation, duties have from the first been levied on certain commodities and are still so levied. We have had a national postoffice, which Prof. Sumner probably admits to be a success; and we have state, if not national, education. Other forms of state action are demanded, among which are those against certain monopolies, particularly those of transportation.[18]

Ward characterized conservatives and their ideas in this manner:

> They feel that practice is running counter to theory. *Laissez faire* has with them become a creed, and they feel as do religious devotees when they see their faith breaking down and their creed superseded by a more liberal and progressive one. They have already long ago said all there is to say. They can now only protest, threaten, and vituperate.[19]

Richard T. Ely

In his attacks on Social Darwinism, Lester Frank Ward was not a lone voice in the wilderness. He had plenty of

[18] Ibid., p. 302.
[19] Ibid., p. 303.

scholarly company; one of the more prominent scholars was the economist Richard T. Ely. Ely, as well as other young economists in the 1880's and 1890's, castigated the followers of classical economics for their dogmatism and simplicity, insisting that traditional economic thought could not cope with the vast changes industrialization had brought about. According to Ely, traditional economists' blind faith in laissez faire and their nearly total acceptance of self-interest as an explanation of human behavior did not fit the complex American society of the late 1800's. "The idea that a business is a man's own and ought not to be interfered with by the public," he wrote,

> is one that belongs to [the] early part of the industrial stage, and it has been only with extreme slowness and obstinacy that it is coming to be recognized by businessmen that such an attitude is an anachronism. Unquestionably the dispute between labor and capital has been aggravated by this fact. Education can do much here to make the transitions easier, because when men recognize the inevitableness of change, they are much less apt to resist it.[20]

Ely foresaw the imposition of many restrictions on private property and greater expansion of public ownership. The creation of national parks, public forest lands, community parks and libraries, and the growing trend toward municipal ownership of public utilities all pointed in this new direction. In addition, Ely argued that private property would more and more be regarded as a public trust and not merely something an individual could use as he wished.

Like most economists of his time, Ely upheld competition as a permanent and necessary feature of human society, but he deplored unequal competition—for example, the "competition" between industrial employers who could combine to fix wages and unorganized workers with only one job market in which to offer their labor. Ely was not a socialist; he looked upon government as an instrument to guard the public interest and insure fair competition.

[20] Richard T. Ely, *Studies in the Evolution of Industrial Society* (New York: Macmillan Co., 1909), p. 61.

> It is at this point important to make a distinction too often overlooked; namely, the radical difference between that socialistic extension of governmental activity which has in view the suppression of competition, and that conservative demand for an extension of governmental activity which has in view the maintenance of competition.[21]

"Scientifically," Ely went on to say,

> the alternative of socialism is our complex socio-economic order, which is based, in the main, upon private property in capital, that is to say, the instruments of production, together with competition in industry. Alongside of competition, however, we have combinations aiming to restrain competition, and we have the beginning of the social regulation of combinations, which will undoubtedly be carried farther in the general interest. Alongside of private production we have a limited amount of governmental

The New York Public Library

Workers making tin cans to be used in packing meats, about 1878.

[21] Ibid., p. 145.

> production. Our various governments—national, state, and local—are clearly destined to extend their productive activities, particularly in the field of monopolies. No one who has eyes to see what is going on throughout the regions of industrial civilization can well doubt this fact. Then we have, too, a distribution, through governmental agency, of a large amount of the wealth produced. A considerable percentage of the population, even now, consists of those who hold public office of one kind or another, and whose salaries are determined by law, and then we have also the activities of government in education and charities, which dispose of a very appreciable proportion of the wealth annually produced. Our social system, then, is a highly complex one, which has been in process of development for centuries. This system, with all its potentialities, is the scientific alternative of socialism.[22]

Many economic and political thinkers of the time paid more attention to the role of religion and religious ethics in society than do their modern counterparts. Frank Lester Ward was an agnostic and saw little value in religion; in fact, Ward considered organized religion and its dogma a barrier to man's progress. Both Ely and Sumner, however, expressed a belief in a divine creator, although they disagreed about what the divine creator had in mind for human society. Sumner argued that individualism was a high Christian ideal, and unfettered competition a positive moral good. Ely, on the other hand, considered individualism without restraint an immoral thing:

> Christian morality is the only stable basis for a State professedly Christian. An ethical demand of the present age is a clearer percentage of the duties of property, intelligence, and social position. It must be recognized that extreme individualism is immoral. Extreme individualism is social anarchy . . . [and] the first social anarchist was Cain, who asked indignantly if he were his brother's keeper. *Laissez faire* policies assure us we are not keepers of our brothers, that each one best promotes the general interest by promoting his own. There are those who tell us in the

[22] Ibid., pp. 468–469.

> name of science, that there is no duty which one class owes to another, and that the nations of the earth are mere collections of individuals, with no reciprocal rights and duties. It is time for right-thinking persons, and particularly for those who profess Christianity, to protest vigorously . . . against such doctrines wherever found.[23]

Ely faulted ministers for not taking a greater interest in the working class and for not upholding the side of labor against capital:

> First, these church leaders are so far away from the toiling masses that they fail to understand their desires, and the motives of their action. I meet few clergymen who, even when they want to be friendly, can give an intelligent statement of the side of labor in any of its many controversies with capital. They rarely converse with leaders of the workingmen, and perhaps more rarely read any labor paper. If they loved the masses, they would instinctively draw near enough to know their aims and motives. Christ moved among the masses and understood them. . . .
>
> Second, the failure to rebuke wickedness in high places is noticed. When you go into a church on Fifth Avenue in New York, rarely, if ever, do you hear the corrupt methods by which the masses have been robbed, and prominent people made millionaires, described and denounced with righteous indignation. When not a workingman is present, the wicked labor agitators are lashed with fury. . . . If the aim were to draw men together, those who minister to congregations made up of employers would so put the case of their employees that it could be understood, and would say everything favorable which could be said in their behalf. . . .
>
> Third, the negative attitude of the Church with respect to every proposed reform discourages, disgusts, and even angers, workingmen. The religious press is concerned with the "errors of socialism". . . and, in short, the errors of any one who proposes anything positive. "The errors of socialism!" Why talk about them? Are they a living issue?

[23] Richard T. Ely, *The Labor Movement in America* (New York: Macmillan Co., 1905), p. 311.

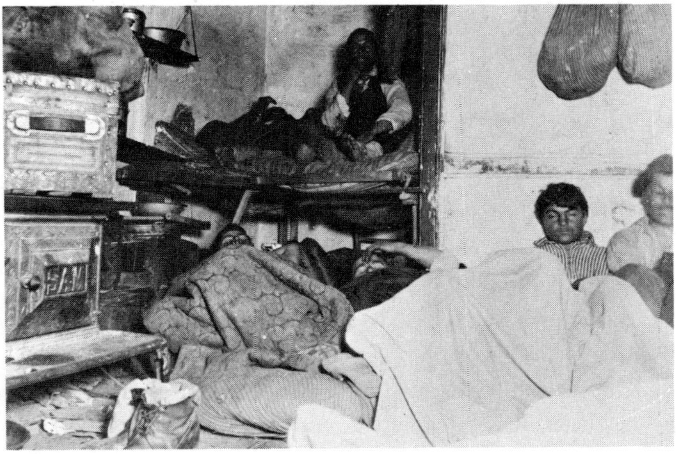

Library of Congress

A room in a New York City tenement, photographed by Jacob Riis about 1890. The men were mostly job-hunting immigrants who paid five cents a night for sleeping space on the floor.

> Is there the slightest danger that they will not be sufficiently discussed? There is about as much prospect of a realization of the socialist's dream in our day, as there is that New Hampshire farmers will harvest their grain in January. . . . If we could hear something about the "the truths of socialism". . . it would be far more to the point. . . .[24]

Ely's criticism did not apply to all ministers. A number of them had concluded that something was awry in American society and that the churches should play a greater role in righting social wrongs. This attitude fostered what came to be known as the social gospel, of which Washington Gladden was an outstanding practitioner.

Washington Gladden

A Congregational minister in Columbus, Ohio, and a former school teacher, Washington Gladden was more a practical man than a philosopher. He was an activist who believed that churches had not lived up to their purpose and social responsibilities.

[24] Richard T. Ely, *The Social Aspects of Christianity* (New York: Thomas Y. Crowell, 1889), pp. 42–44.

Gladden believed that if men followed the true teachings of Jesus, social and industrial conditions would be vastly improved. He also believed that government had a clear role to play in a "Christian State." He advocated government control of natural monopolies—railroads, telegraph companies, street railways, gas companies, and electric companies—which by their nature should not be competitive. Gladden was particularly eager for close government regulation of railroads:

> The great business of railway transportation never will be managed well upon competitive principles. I judge that it never will be, because, as a matter of history, it never has been. It is essentially a monopoly; and the attempt to force it under the law of competition must result in economic wreck and moral ruin. It is a monopoly, and a monopoly which the government must either own or firmly control. This is the goal ahead of us; the sooner we clearly see it and shape our course to reach it, the better for our peace. . . .[25]

Gladden, however, did not wish to be tarred by the socialist brush. There were, he agreed, certain merits in socialist principles and advantages in socialistic programs, but he feared that their application would result in restrictions on personal liberty. This danger outweighed any benefits they might bring.

Unlike William Graham Sumner, Washington Gladden believed in free will, by which he meant that man had the power to order his environment as he pleased, that he was not a helpless pawn of natural laws and forces. Wrote Gladden in 1897:

> We must start in political economy with the doctrines of freedom of the will; and we must believe communities as well as men can do what they ought to do; that the intelligence and the conscience of any community can assail and remove recognized evils. We are not hopelessly drifting in the current of social progress; we may shape our

[25] Washington Gladden, *Social Facts and Forces* (New York: G. P. Putnam's Sons, 1897), p. 148.

own course. . . . Civilization does not grow wild; it is not a natural product; it is a product of the finest of the arts; it is the work of reason and conscience and benevolence.[26]

Unregulated corporate activities and monopoly caught severe criticism from Gladden. The baleful influence of corporations, he believed, was undermining public morality:

> I believe that the influence of the corporation, *as it now exists*, upon public vigor and public morality is decidedly injurious. For the advantages that we secure by means of the system of corporate industry we are paying a large price. If the effect of the employment of this agency is to lower the standards of commercial morality, to increase social inequalities, and to repress the individuality, the self-reliance, and the enterprise of the people, there is certainly a heavy deduction to be made from the gains they bring us. . . . And it is precisely these subtle but deep-working forces that the ordinary student of statistics and finance is pretty sure to miss. Triumphant Democracy, counting its millions of population and its billions of wealth, reciting the enormous gains of its manufacturers, its mines, its farms, footing up its thousands of miles of railroads, and boasting of the swiftness of its trains and the cheapness of its transportation, takes very little note of these effects upon the intelligence, the morality, the self-respect of the masses of the people. The fact that a period may be reached "when wealth accumulates and men decay," is a fact that your enthusiastic statitician ignores.[27]

Government regulation, according to Gladden, was the only means by which the subtly destructive influence of corporations could be overcome.

Gladden upheld the right of workers to combine—unionize—to protect their interests and achieve better wages and working conditions. Only employers of little intelligence, he said, denied this right:

> The first condition of successful arbitration is an unreserved and ungrudging admission on the part of employers

[26] Ibid., pp. 2–3.
[27] Ibid., pp. 100–101.

> of the right of the men to combine, and a clear recognition of the fact that the men stand upon an equal footing with themselves in the whole negotiation. It is very hard for many employers to recognize this right of the laborers to combine. The fact that these combinations of laborers often misuse their power; that they make unreasonable and injurious demands, and strike for foolish reasons, and sometimes resort to violence, is not to be denied. But if the abuse of privilege is a reason for the refusal of privilege, the right of capital to combine might, I think, be seriously questioned. Have we never heard of companies and corporations using their power selfishly and tyrannically?[28]

Gladden concluded that "the attempt to deprive [workers] of the right to stand together for their own defense is one that [workers] ought to resist by all lawful means," and he promised labor a good deal of moral support:

> They ought to know that all men who hate oppression are on their side. It is little to say that they ought to win in this struggle; they will win, and they must win. There never can be honorable and enduring peace between these classes until the right of the workmen to combine for their own protection is cordially and unreservedly conceded by their employers.[29]

Gladden also supported the abolition of child labor, government regulation of working hours, especially for women, and tighter compulsory education laws.

As a social reformer, Gladden appealed to Christians to unite in concerted action to bring about better social and economic conditions. He believed that the welfare of the Christian church was bound to the welfare of the toiling masses and that the church should be the leading institution for social change. Gladden stated that when the church lived up to the teachings of Jesus Christ "it will save its own life and that of the nation with whose destiny it is put in trust."[30]

[28] Ibid., p. 163.

[29] Ibid., p. 66.

[30] Washington Gladden, *The Church and Modern Life* (Boston: Houghton Mifflin, 1908), p. 147.

When he chose, Washington Gladden could be very specific in his criticism. The American Board of Commissioners for Foreign Missions received his condemnation when it solicited and received a $100,000 gift from John D. Rockefeller, president of Standard Oil, a corporation that controlled the production and distribution of over ninety percent of the nation's oil and oil products. Gladden characterized the money as "tainted" and said that its acceptance made the church a partner with "plunderers." Such statements did not endear him to wealthy churchgoers or corporation executives. They firmly believed that Rockefeller and others who had accumulated great wealth were doing God's work, that they were, as God intended, making full use of their talents. And the proof of God's pleasure in them was the wealth he had blessed them with.

Walter Rauschenbusch

Walter Rauschenbusch, who in 1902 became a professor of church history at the Rochester Theological Seminary in Rochester, New York, was another prominent advocate of the social gospel. Educated in Europe, Rauschenbusch enjoyed a reputation as an intellectual, yet he was well acquainted with the conditions under which common people lived. Beginning in 1886, he had served as pastor of the Second German Baptist Church in New York City, a church of impoverished German immigrants. His congregation suffered dreadfully during the depression of 1893, and this experience had a deep influence on him. He emerged as the social gospel's most effective spokesman.

Walter Rauschenbusch.

The New York Public Library

"We are assured that the poor are poor through their own faults," he once wrote,

> that rent and profits are the just dues of foresight and ability; that the immigrants are the cause of corruption in our city politics; that we cannot compete with foreign countries unless our working class will descend to the wages paid abroad. These are all very plausible assertions, but they are lies dressed up in truth. There is a great deal of conscious lying. Industrialism as a whole sends out deceptive prospectuses just like single corporations within it.

> But in the main these misleading theories are the complacent self-deception of those who profit by present conditions and are loath to believe that their life is working harm.[31]

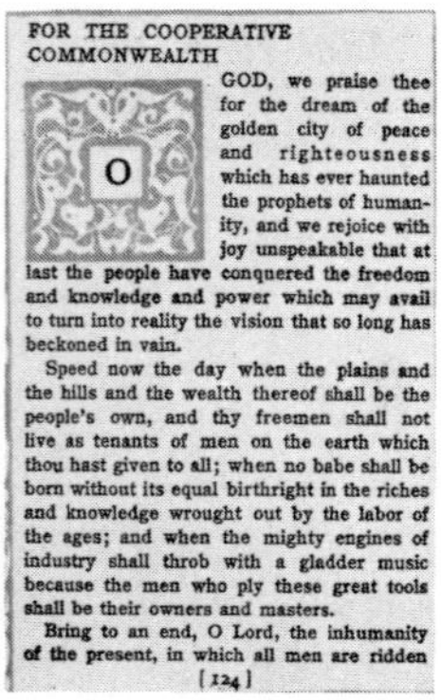

FOR THE COOPERATIVE COMMONWEALTH

O GOD, we praise thee for the dream of the golden city of peace and righteousness which has ever haunted the prophets of humanity, and we rejoice with joy unspeakable that at last the people have conquered the freedom and knowledge and power which may avail to turn into reality the vision that so long has beckoned in vain.

Speed now the day when the plains and the hills and the wealth thereof shall be the people's own, and thy freemen shall not live as tenants of men on the earth which thou hast given to all; when no babe shall be born without its equal birthright in the riches and knowledge wrought out by the labor of the ages; and when the mighty engines of industry shall throb with a gladder music because the men who ply these great tools shall be their owners and masters.

Bring to an end, O Lord, the inhumanity of the present, in which all men are ridden

[124]

A prayer "for the Cooperative Commonwealth," from Rauschenbusch's book, *Prayers of the Social Awakening.*

Rauschenbusch wished to turn the force of Christianity against the materialism of the new industrial society. He contended that men must be made to realize that they were not serving God in their scramble for money. They must be educated to the fact that they were indulging in self-deception. As he explained,

> If a man sacrifices his human dignity and self-respect to increase his income, or stunts his intellectual growth and his human affections to swell his bank account, he is to that extent serving mammon and denying God. Likewise if he uses up and injures the life of his fellow-men to make money for himself, he serves mammon and denies God. But our industrial order does both. It makes property the end, and man the means to produce it.[32]

A society that treated men as machines to produce things would, Rauschenbusch feared, eventually be visited by violent class conflict. To avert such a catastrophe, he said, the churches must take an active part in reforming society. Ministers must act as buffers and interpreters between rich and poor, capital and labor:

> A minister mingling with both classes can act as an interpreter to both. He can soften the increasing class hatred of the working class. He can infuse the spirit of moral enthusiasm into the economic struggle of the dispossessed and lift it to something more than a "stomach question." On the other hand, among the well-to-do, he can strengthen the consciousness that the working people have a real grievance and so increase the disposition to make concessions in practical cases and check the inclination to resort to force for the suppression of discontent. If the ministry

[31] Walter Rauschenbusch, *Christianity and the Social Crisis* (New York: Macmillan Co., 1911), pp. 350–351.

[32] Ibid., p. 369.

would awaken among the wealthy a sense of social compunction and moral uneasiness, that alone might save our nation from a revolutionary explosion.[33]

Rauschenbusch's main purpose was to "Christianize" industrial society. This he considered simply a humanizing process:

> Christianizing the social order means bringing it into harmony with the ethical convictions which we identify with Christ. A fairly definite body of moral convictions has taken shape in modern humanity. They express our collective conscience, our working religion. The present social order denies and flouts many of these principles of our ethical life and compels us in practice to outrage our better self. We demand therefore that the moral sense of humanity shall be put in control and shall be allowed to reshape the institutions of social life.[34]

Rauschenbusch offered the following conditions for the development of a truly Christianized society:

> If production could be organized on a basis of cooperative fraternity; if distribution could at least approximately be determined by justice; if all men could be conscious that their labor contributed to the welfare of all and that their personal well-being was dependent on the prosperity of the Commonwealth; if predatory business and parasitic wealth ceased and all men lived only by their labor; if the luxury of unearned wealth no longer made us all feverish with covetousness and a simpler life became the fashion; if our time and strength were not used up either in getting a bare living or in amassing unusable wealth and we had more leisure for the higher pursuits of the mind and the soul—then there might be a chance to live such a life of gentleness and brotherly kindness and tranquility of heart that Jesus desired for men.[35]

[33] Ibid., p. 368.

[34] Walter Rauschenbusch, *Christianizing the Social Order* (New York: Macmillan Co., 1914), pp. 18–19.

[35] Ibid., p. 341.

To many people Walter Rauschenbusch sounded like a socialist, but he disavowed the label, regarding socialism as no less materialistic than industrial capitalism. The majority of social gospelists believed that socialism could never solve the problems of America's industrial society.

Edward Bellamy

Edward Bellamy was the son of a Baptist minister in Chicopee Falls, Massachusetts; except for several trips to Europe, he lived most of his life in that state. He first became concerned about social problems during his European travels, observing that these problems plagued Europeans as well as Americans. Although Bellamy studied law, a literary career held the strongest appeal for him and it was as a novelist that he made his greatest contributions to American thought. His novel *Looking Backward*, a raging bestseller published in 1888, was especially influential.

Arguing for a utopian socialistic society, *Looking Backward* presented a romantic picture of America in the year 2000, by which time machines had lifted the heavy and wearying tasks of labor from men. In this utopia the state—the national government—directed all the activities of production and distribution and guaranteed the security of all individuals. According to Bellamy, it was the absence of competition among the citizens of the new society that caused this Garden of Eden to flourish. Competition was no longer a necessary ingredient in human life, for everyone had all he needed or wanted.

As the book achieved popularity, Bellamy clubs were formed throughout the world and their members met periodically to discuss the social implications of Bellamy's work. He himself actively supported these organizations, believing that the conversion of a capitalistic society to utopian socialism was a distinct possibility in the near future. He was wrong. Despite its temporary appeal, the movement was a complete failure as a political force. Many critics decried Bellamy's socialism and others complained that his idea that competition would ever cease to be a vital factor in human relations was wholly unrealistic. Still others saw Bellamy's utopia only as a totalitarian state devoid of human liberty. Although Bellamy took a hand in spreading his ideas, he was not a political activist. Like many intellectual leaders of the period, he distrusted politics and took little part in them.

Henry George

Edward Bellamy put his faith in government-administered technology as a means of alleviating social ills. Henry George had a more immediate and simpler solution.

Henry George had tried his hand at many jobs—seaman, delivery boy, gold prospector, clerk, typesetter, salesman, journalist, editor—and failed at all of them. Then, during the depression of the 1870's, he wrote *Progress and Poverty* and assured himself a place in history books.

Wealth-producing power, George wrote, had increased tremendously, and one would expect that as a consequence poverty would have disappeared. Yet this was far from being the case.

> We plow new fields, we open new mines, we found new cities, we drive back the Indian and exterminate the buffalo; we girdle the land with iron roads and lace the air with telegraph wires; we add knowledge to knowledge, and utilize invention after invention. . . . Yet it becomes no easier for the masses of our people to make a living. On the contrary, it is becoming harder. . . . The gulf between the employed and the employer is growing wider; social contrasts are becoming sharper; as liveried carriages appear, so do barefooted children.[36]

Once there had been seemingly limitless opportunity in America because land was plentiful and cheap; the vast public domain offered nearly everyone a chance to be free and independent and equal. But gradually the public domain had disappeared and industrialization had speeded the process of concentrating wealth in the hands of a few, bringing social stratification and diminishing opportunity for the masses of the people.

[36] Henry George, *Progress and Poverty* (New York: Robert Schalkenbach Foundation, 1955), p. 5.

Much of the wealth held by a few individuals, as far as George could see, resulted not so much from production as from higher and higher land values. Land became scarce, for example, as communities grew, and the owners of land thus got richer. But such profits were wholly unearned. They resulted from speculation or good fortune, not from productive labor. George proposed that profits from the sale of land be taxed at 100 percent; this would have an equalizing effect among classes and with this source of income no government would need additional taxation—hence the term "single tax," which has since been associated with Henry George. "I do not propose," he wrote,

> either to purchase or to confiscate private property in land. The first would be unjust; the second needless. Let the individuals who now hold it still retain, if they want to, possession of what they are pleased to call *their* land. Let them buy and sell, and bequeath and divide it. We may safely leave them the shell, if we take the kernel. *It is not necessary to confiscate land; it is only necessary to confiscate rent* [the difference between the buying and selling price of land].[37]

Men who owned valuable real estate in such cities as New York or in new and developing communities—whose real estate value might increase dramatically within a brief span of years—were not enthusiastic about George's single tax. Nor were farmers who improved their land expecting its value to increase. But to landless city dwellers, the poor and the working class, and to men who devoted their lives to the labor union movement, Henry George made a great deal of sense. The utter simplicity of a single tax on land appealed to them. It would have a social and economic leveling effect they could not help but applaud. Without land themselves, they could not fail to benefit from the single tax.

Henry George was not merely a theoretician. In 1886, backed by labor organizations and numerous intellectuals, he ran for the office of mayor of New York. He lost, and

[37] Ibid., p. 405.

Brown Brothers

In addition to a single tax on land, Henry George advocated unqualified free trade and public ownership of utilities.

despite extremely poor health he ran again ten years later. This time, shortly after making a campaign speech at the Central Opera House, he collapsed and died.

Progress and Poverty, published in 1879, sold over three million copies. It sparked the formation of Land and Labor clubs to spread the doctrine of the single tax. The idea stirred a great deal of interest—and controversy—but nothing came of it, although the concept of inheritance taxes might owe something to Henry George. George has been called one of the few truly original economic thinkers of all time, but his ideas were much too radical for his or any other age to accept. "We should reach the ideal of the socialist," he wrote in *Progress and Poverty*,

> but not through government repression. Government would change its character, and would become the administration

> of a great co-operative society. It would become merely the agency by which the common property was administered for the common benefit.[38]

And in a later book, *Social Problems,* he wrote:

> The primary purpose and end of government being to secure the natural rights and equal liberty of each, all businesses that are in their very nature monopolies become properly the functions of the state. As society develops, the state must assume these functions, in their nature cooperative, in order to secure the equal rights and liberty of all. . . . It is the business of government to do for the mass of individuals those things which cannot be done, or cannot be so well done, by individual action.[39]

These, then, were some of the voices of acclaim and dissent that industrialization stimulated in nineteenth-century America. Most were those of intellectuals and only a few of them—like Henry George—were activists as well as theoreticians. Another group—composed of those who caused the changes that men like Sumner or Gladden applauded or decried—were mainly doers. They rationalized their behavior when challenged, but for the most part they were content to act, building what they believed to be a better America. These were the businessmen, financiers, and industrialists of the age.

[38] Ibid., pp. 456–457.

[39] Henry George, *Social Problems* (New York: Robert Schalkenbach Foundation, 1953), pp. 176–177.

SUGGESTED READINGS

Bellamy, Edward. *Looking Backward.* New American Library, Signet Books.

Hofstadter, Richard. *Social Darwinism in American Thought.* Beacon Press.

Rauschenbusch, Walter. *Christianity and the Social Crisis.* Harper & Row, Torchbooks.

Sheldon, Charles M. *In His Steps.* Pyramid.

Smith, Adam. *Selections from the Wealth of Nations.* Edited by G. J. Stigler. Appleton-Century-Crofts.

Sumner, William Graham. *Folkways.* New American Library, Mentor Books.

Sumner, William Graham. *What Social Classes Owe to Each Other.* Caxton.

Ward, Lester Frank. *Lester Frank Ward.* Edited by I. Gerver. Thomas Y. Crowell.

Culver Pictures

The power wielded by the great industrialists of the late nineteenth century is only slightly exaggerated in this 1882 cartoon, which shows Cornelius Vanderbilt, Cyrus Field, Jay Gould, Russell Sage, and other "robber barons" dividing up the United States and negotiating for the purchase of Europe. The cartoon's caption reads, "Let Them Have It All, and Be Done With It!"

THE INDUSTRIALISTS

The many changes that occurred in nineteenth-century America can be represented with statistics on growing rates of production, miles of railroads built, population movements from farm to city, occupational shifts from agricultural to factory work, or countless other manifestations of a developing industrial society. But the age is perhaps best symbolized by the careers of the men who presided over these changes—the great industrialists and the financiers, the new millionaires who amassed great fortunes and came to dominate the American economy through the enterprises they headed.

Neither contemporary observers nor historians have agreed in their assessments of such powerful business leaders as John D. Rockefeller, John Pierpont Morgan, Cornelius Vanderbilt, and others who rose to prominence in the nineteenth century. Playing on the phrase "the Era of Good Feelings"—an often-used historical label for the period following the War of 1812—one writer has characterized the late nineteenth century as "the Era of Good Stealings."[1] The tag "robber barons" has been pinned on industrial magnates by those who have seen them as unscrupulous rascals who corrupted politicians and robbed or exploited competitors, investors, consumers, and workers. Counterviews have stressed the constructive accomplishments of America's great entrepreneurs and have tended to employ positive designations like "captains of industry" and " industrial statesmen."

[1]Thomas A. Bailey, *The American Pageant: A History of the Republic* (Boston: D. C. Heath, 1956), p. 485.

Late nineteenth-century reformers sometimes used the term "robber barons" in their attacks on big business, but historian Hal Bridges has credited Matthew Josephson with making the term standard in American historical writing. In his 1934 study of the great tycoons, *The Robber Barons: The Great American Capitalists*, Josephson contended that industrialism had destroyed traditional power relationships in American society. The new industrialists became the new centers of power and influence, and in using this power they were guided solely by a ruthless desire to make money. Any benefits that accrued to society as a result of the industrialists' activities—such as increased production of goods and services—were simply incidental to this overriding desire for making money. In Josephson's view, the robber barons were merciless destroyers of competition; they were not, as they so often claimed, upholders of the free-enterprise system. Josephson believed that the monopolies they built contributed directly to the increasing poverty, crime, political corruption, and other ills that plagued the age in which they lived.

Allan Nevins' sympathetic biography of John D. Rockefeller exemplifies the favorable approach to the careers of America's great business leaders. As Nevins saw it, Rockefeller was driven by more than a simple lust for wealth; he and others like him were striving for "competitive achievement, self-expression, and the imposition of their wills on a given environment."[2] They simply responded to challenge and adventure in the same way that has prompted the most able men in all walks of life and in all ages to attempt to rise above their contemporaries. They were, in short, playing life's "Great Game," and one should not fault them because they succeeded so well. Rockefeller himself was obsessed by a desire to impose order on the chaotic oil industry, where ruinous competition had been accompanied by incredible inefficiency. He and his counterparts in other industries transformed a wasteful and frag-

[2] Allan Nevins, *John D. Rockefeller: The Heroic Age of American Enterprise,* 2 vols. (New York: Charles Scribner's Sons, 1940), 2: 714.

mented business environment into an economy of large and efficient industrial units. Rather than indict them for the ruthlessness of their methods, Nevins believed, people today should thank the industrialists for their creative accomplishments. Had it not been for their leadership, the United States would not have become a great industrial power and its people would not enjoy the highest standard of living in the world. Furthermore, without their contributions to the process of industrialization, "the free world might have lost the First World War and most certainly would have lost the Second."[3] To Nevins and other like-minded historians, Josephson's robber barons were great industrial statesmen who played a significant role in saving the world from totalitarianism.

Neither version—robber barons or industrial statesmen—tells the whole story. It can be safely said that the robber-baron stereotype fails to account for differences in character or for the constructive accomplishments and possibly upright motives of many businessmen. As Hal Bridges has observed:

> In an emotional, romanticized way, this concept sums up the business activities of Jay Gould and his kind and expresses the predatory side of the careers of many other business leaders of the post-Civil War era. But it grants insufficient recognition to the creative aspects of such careers or to business leaders of habitually high moral standards. It tends to deny to business leaders through thirty-five years of American life that basic capacity for doing good as well as evil which historians freely concede to other members of the human race.[4]

On the other hand, to justify morally reprehensible methods by unforeseen long-range results is not necessarily an ac-

[3] Allan Nevins, *Study in Power: John D. Rockefeller, Industrialist and Philanthropist,* 2 vols. (New York: Charles Scribner's Sons, 1953), 1: viii–ix.

[4] Quoted in Abraham S. Eisenstadt, ed., *American History: Recent Interpretations,* 2 vols. (New York: Thomas Y. Crowell, 1961), 2: 103.

ceptable practice. Historian Carl Degler put it this way:

> To defend the methods of these leaders on the ground that the job was done, as some historians have, is to be guilty of justifying the ends by the means. But to go even further as Allan Nevins has, to justify them and their methods on the ground that the industrial power they built enabled the United States to win two world wars, is to commit the more grievous crime of excusing men in the name of consequences they never intended. Such a procedure drains the whole matter of moral content.[5]

The remainder of this chapter sketches the careers of a few of the better-known giants of American industry. The lives of these men are sufficiently representative of the period to give a picture of both the more flagrant abuses and the positive achievements associated with the time.

Jay Gould

A small group of railroad speculators has often been singled out as a prototype of the robber-baron concept. Among the supreme crooks, Daniel Drew, Jim Fisk, and Jay Gould comprise an unholy triumvirate that has drawn the most severe historical criticism. Men like J. P. Morgan, John D. Rockefeller, and Andrew Carnegie, are, in spite of some of their questionable practices, usually regarded at least as innovators and builders. Drew, Fisk, and Gould, however, have usually been looked upon as wreckers. And, if one were to select from this group the classic villain, the greatest wrecker of them all, that distinction would surely go to Jay Gould. Gustavus Myers is typical of other writers in his assessment of Gould:

> His career from 1867 onward stood out in the fullest prominence; a multitude of official reports and investigations and court records contribute a translucent record. He became invested with a sinister distinction as the most cold-blooded corruptionist, spoilator, and financial pirate

[5] Carl Degler, *Out of Our Past: The Forces That Shaped Modern America* (New York: Harper & Row, 1959), p. 249.

Culver Pictures

Wall Street—"Jay Gould's Private Bowling Alley."

> of his time; and so thoroughly did he earn this reputation that to the end of his days it confronted him at every step, and survived to become the standing reproach and terror of his descendants. For nearly half a century the very name of Jay Gould was a persisting jeer and byword, an object of popular contumely and hatred, the signification of every foul and base crime by which greed triumphs.[6]

Gould was born May 27, 1836, in Roxbury, New York, the son of a poor farmer. A small man and physically weak, he seems to have compensated for these deficiencies by developing at an early age an exceptional talent for making money. He worked for a blacksmith and as a clerk in a country store to obtain funds for an education at the local academy, or high school, where he acquired a working knowledge of surveying. Then, for three years, he worked at preparing maps for several New York counties. By the

[6] Gustavus Myers, *The History of the Great American Fortunes* (New York: Random House, 1936), p. 397.

time he reached twenty-one, Gould had saved $5,000 and was eager to build on this small fortune. He opened a tannery in northern Pennsylvania in partnership with a New York leather merchant. When the merchant committed suicide a few years later, many people blamed Gould's sharp business practices—there was evidence that Gould had been quietly fleecing him.

Abandoning the tannery, Gould turned to the more profitable endeavor of speculating in railroads; by the 1860's, he was engaged in such speculation on a grand scale. In October, 1867, Gould and Jim Fisk joined the board of directors of the Erie Railroad. They had been brought in by Daniel Drew, the company's treasurer.

Drew had made his start in the business world as an imaginative cattle drover. When driving his animals to market, he deliberately kept them thirsty until they were almost there. Then he let them drink their fill, inflating their weight and thus their sale price, and contributing a new phrase to the lexicon of business—"watered stock," which later came to mean stock market shares issued at a higher price than the company's assets or earnings warranted. Speculation in railroads and steamship lines made Drew a very wealthy man. He had become an officer of the Erie as a consequence of a $3 million loan he made the railroad after the panic of 1857—he had taken 58,000 shares of stock as collateral.

Cornelius Vanderbilt.

Brown Brothers

Cornelius Vanderbilt also had a deep interest in the Erie. Known as "the Commodore," Vanderbilt had begun his career as a Staten Island ferry boy and had made his initial wealth from steamship lines and stock speculation. During the 1860's he invested heavily in railroads and finally gained control of the following three railroads: the Harlem, which ran into New York City; the Hudson, with tracks along the west bank of the river between New York City and Albany; and the New York Central, which by 1865 extended from New York City to Toledo, Ohio. Vanderbilt hoped to add lines that would lead into Chicago. The Erie was moving in the same direction and he had his eye on that railroad, wishing to control it.

In 1866, Vanderbilt bought 20,000 shares of Erie stock

and got on the Erie board of directors. Then he quietly bought more stock, finding, however, that the supply seemed inexhaustible. Vanderbilt did not know it, but Daniel Drew was issuing new Erie shares faster than Vanderbilt could acquire them. Drew also fed into the market 30,000 of the 58,000 shares he had taken as collateral on his loan to the railroad, all the while contracting to sell stock at the high price to which Vanderbilt's bullishness and attempt to corner Erie shares had driven it. The following account of the episode's outcome is from *The Book of Daniel Drew*, written by the old man himself:

> Erie was then at 95, and promised to go still higher. People reckoned that I was a reckless plunger. The weeks ran along. Pretty soon it came time for me to deliver. The price held strong at 95. My enemies began to snicker. They said I was cornered. But I took the twenty-eight thousand shares I had kept up my sleeve, and dumped them into the market all at once. It was probably the biggest surprise Wall Street up to that time had known. Prices were knocked into a cocked hat. Erie gave one plunge—fell to 47. Which means, I made the other fellow pay me $95 a share for stock which was costing me now only $47. So I cleaned up $48 on every share dealt in. It was the finest scoop I had ever made. It is true, those shares had been intrusted to me only to hold as security until the road should pay back my loan. But in a business deal, you can't stop for every little technicality.[7]

What Drew had done was at least slightly illegal, but that did not bother Vanderbilt nearly so much as the fact that he had been badly taken. The incident made him determined to purge Drew from the Erie's directorate. To do this he still had to acquire the majority of Erie stock.

Vanderbilt began once again to buy Erie shares. At the same time he obtained a court injunction prohibiting the railroad from issuing new stock. Defying the injunction,

[7] Bouch White, ed., *The Book of Daniel Drew* (New York: Doubleday, Doran & Co., 1910), p. 212.

Gould threw 50,000 new shares of Erie stock on the market, making it practically impossible for the Commodore's plan to succeed. Although Gould, Drew, and Fisk were forced to flee to Jersey City to avoid prosecution, they did foil Vanderbilt's attempt to gain control of the Erie. Later, by bribing enough legislators in the state capital at Albany, Fisk managed to have Gould's new stock issue legalized. While Gould and Fisk celebrated their victory over Vanderbilt, Drew secretly compromised with the Commodore so that he might return to New York without having to answer contempt charges for disobeying the injunction. Gould and Fisk considered Drew's action a betrayal and within a few months they forced him out of the Erie. Later they got charges against themselves quashed. Wrote Drew:

> It's a sorry colt that will kick its own dam. I felt all the more sore at the unfeeling way in which Gould and Fisk were treating me in this matter, because I had been their foster parent, so to speak. When they came into Wall Street as yearlings, I had taken them up—had showed them how to make money. And now, for them to turn on me in my old age and strip me in this way, was an unthankful thing to do. It was like a mare of mine once, that got a stone in her feet. So I got off and started to help her. As I was bending over the hoof and trying to dig the stone out, she reached down and bit me in the seat. I remembered it made me very sore towards her—this ungrateful act of hers. So in the present case. I felt I had never seen a more ungrateful pair of men than Jim Fisk and Jay Gould.[8]

However ungrateful they might have been, it was apparent that Fisk and Gould had learned quickly and well from their "foster parent." So well, in fact, that when their work was done the Erie was under their complete control.

Fisk and Gould were as dissimilar in appearance and life style as they were similar in business ethics. The diminutive and consumptive Gould was a serious and devoted family man. "Jubilee Jim" Fisk was a 300-pound playboy who enjoyed horse racing and "cuddlesome women." It was

[8] Ibid., p. 375.

Fisk who moved the Erie's headquarters to a New York opera house, where he played at being an impresario. But both men seemed to view every business they entered as fit only for exploitation. Gustavus Myers described how they looted the Erie Railroad after it fell under their control:

> Between 1868 and 1873 Gould and his accomplices had issued $64,000,000 of watered stock. Gould, so the Erie books revealed, had charged $12,000,000 as representing the outlay for construction and equipment, yet not a new rail had been laid, nor a new engine put to use, nor a new station built. These twelve millions or more were what he and his immediate accomplices had taken outright from the Erie Railroad treasury. Considerable sums were, of course, paid corruptly to politicians, but Gould got them all back, as well as the plunder of his associates, by personally manipulating Erie stock so as to compel them to sell at a great loss to themselves, and great profit to himself. Furthermore, in these manipulations of stock, he scooped in more millions from other sources.[9]

Spectacular as Gould's milking of the Erie Railroad was, it pales in comparison to his attempt to corner the gold market in 1869. From the beginning of the Civil War, gold had been extremely scarce; by 1869 there was only $15 million worth in actual circulation in the United States. Gould's plan was to get control of all the gold in circulation and fix his own price for it; it did not matter to him that this plan, if it succeeded, would not only cause severe economic problems but would also ruin many businesses. Using the funds he had taken from the Erie, he began to buy gold on the Stock Exchange. Gould's only fear was that the United States Treasury might put some of the gold it kept on reserve into circulation, which would spoil his plan. At the time the government had $95 million in gold reserves, and Gould proceeded to insure that no part of it would be thrown on the market. He intended to influence the government's policies by working through A. R. Corbin,

[9] Myers, *Great American Fortunes,* p. 419.

a brother-in-law of President Ulysses S. Grant. Gould bestowed on Corbin some $2 million worth of gold bonds, assuming that this would give him leverage in the White House. Through Corbin and with the aid of Jim Fisk, Gould even attempted to influence the president directly; although he found he could not depend on Grant for support, he managed to convince many people in Wall Street that high government officials were in collusion with him. This impression was strengthened by newspaper reports stating that the government did not intend to release any gold.

"Jubilee Jim" Fisk.

Culver Pictures

Despite Gould's efforts, a number of financiers remained unconvinced. They suspected that Gould was bluffing and could not really depend on government support, and they spread rumors to this effect. As a consequence of the rumors, the price of gold declined. Gould found himself faced with complete ruin, since he was holding large amounts of gold he had bought at very high prices. But, as one historian has observed, "he hovered again and again on the brink of failure but never once fell over." From this, his boldest venture of all, Gould emerged virtually unscathed. His first step toward extricating himself was to convince Fisk that President Grant was an ally and that all they had to do was to buy more gold. The two men bought a controlling interest in the Tenth National Bank and proceeded to use that institution to issue fraudulent checks in order to make their gold purchases. By September of 1869, Gould, Fisk, and their partners held contracts for more gold than was actually in circulation. The immediate result of their strategy was that banking, manufacturing, and importing interests were forced to borrow at a price dictated by Gould. This situation naturally caused great consternation in business circles, and President Grant decided to release some of the government's gold in order to lower the price. Gould discovered the government's intentions and betrayed his partners by secretly selling gold before the price dropped. Practically everyone was buying gold while Gould was busily disposing of his.

The market opened on September 24, 1869, with bankers, manufacturers, and other business interests instructing their brokers to buy gold at any price. Jim Fisk and Gould's other accomplices were among those still buying. Fisk, in fact, was said to have been running around the Gold Room at the Stock Exchange yelling that the president was in on the deal. Then, early in the afternoon, word arrived that the United States Treasury was selling gold and the whole market collapsed within a few minutes. Many thought Gould had been ruined but his secret sale actually brought him close to $12 million in profits. Through the aid of a corrupt judge, Gould and Fisk managed to repudiate their previous contracts to buy, thus ruining the brokers and speculators who had been riding on the price of gold. As Richard O'Connor has noted:

> Perhaps the most bizarre, almost incredible aspect of the feverish scheme was that the report of the President's corruption could be shouted in the market place, and the only reaction was to shift positions in the Gold Room accordingly. Everyone, apparently, was prepared to believe it and accept it, none to protest or question or demand investigation. This quick and easy acceptance of the rumors about the involvement of the nation's leading military hero, its honest, plodding conqueror of the Southern Confederacy, all taken on the word of a knavish clown, was a true and acute measure of the deadly cynicism which had infected the nation since Appomattox. Everyone was feathering his own nest, why not the President?[10]

According to Charles Francis Adams, a contemporary of Gould and Fisk, "The present evil has its roots deep down in the social organization and springs from a diseased public opinion. Failure seems to be regarded as the one unpardonable crime, success as the all-redeeming virtue, the acquisition of wealth as the single worthy aim of life."[11] If society's supreme value was success in economic undertakings without regard for scruples, then the career of Jay Gould is worth studying as a mirror to the age. As for

[10] Richard O'Connor, *Gould's Millions* (Garden City, N.Y.: Doubleday, 1962), p. 100. Copyright © 1962 by Richard O'Connor. Reprinted by permission of Doubleday & Company, Inc.

[11] Charles Francis Adams, *Chapters of Erie and Other Essays* (New York: Augustus M. Kelly, 1967), p. 41.

President Grant, one historian described him as being

> personally honest, but gullible, naive, politically obtuse, and fanatically loyal to the blowsy, horsy, cigar-smoking crowd that swarmed around him and took full advantage of his befuddlement. The slimy trail of corruption, which directly implicated his brother-in-law, led perilously close to the White House door.[12]

Not only was Grant befuddled but his entire administration often was considered to have been the most incompetent in American history. Thomas A. Bailey concluded in his book entitled *Presidential Greatness* that "Grant was an ignorant and confused President, and his eight long years in blunderland are generally regarded as a national disgrace."[13]

Jay Gould went on to acquire control of several railroad lines in the West, profiting from their government land grants and franchises. He acquired the Pacific Mail Steamship Company, Western Union, new rapid transit lines in New York City, a series of coal mines, some newspapers, and finally railroads in the East to round out, as Matthew Josephson said, "an industrial empire which spread its crazy network from one shore of the continent to the other."

> The railroads, the telegraph lines, the ships, the newspapers, all were part of an imperial plan to capture strategic sections of the country's industrial system and by blocking it first at one point then at another, to levy infinite toll upon it.[14]

Gould warred against labor with even less compassion than he displayed in his dealings with fellow capitalists. Frequently he reduced wages, seemingly daring his workers to fight back. In 1884 and 1885 he was plagued by bloody and destructive strikes organized by the Knights of Labor. Gould was forced to restore the wage levels of shopmen

[12] Thomas A. Bailey, *Presidential Greatness* (New York: Appleton-Century, 1966), p. 147.

[13] Ibid., p. 295.

[14] Matthew Josephson, *The Robber Barons: The Great American Capitalists* (New York: Harcourt, Brace, 1934), pp. 192–193.

and other railway workers who had been the victims of ten-percent wage reductions. Gould, however, considered all such agreements temporary expedients. In more propitious times he would have his revenge. More than any other single individual Gould was responsible for distorting the public image of the labor movement. According to Myers, Gould's most successful and insidious method of influencing public opinion

> was by his control of the Western Union Telegraph Company, and, through that corporation, of the Associated Press, the foremost news distributing agency in the United States. Distorted, misleading or false news dispatches were manufactured or artfully colored and supplied to the public press. These not only gave Gould superior underhand facilities for influencing the course of the stock market, but they were also used in favor of capitalists and against labor and radical movements at every opportunity. The public was fed on grossly perverted news accounts of strikes and labor and political movements; upon this fabricated news the newspaper owners, themselves capitalists or largely servile to capital, based hostile if not malevolent editorials; and the combination of the whole was used to prejudice the mass of the public against any movement or agitation threatening the complete sway of capital.[15]

Gould died in 1892, leaving a fortune of $72 million.

"Jubilee Jim" Fisk met a violent end, all because of a "cuddlesome" woman. His mistress of many years, Josie Mansfield, became infatuated with a young man named Edward S. "Ned" Stokes, and together they began to blackmail Fisk, using as bait compromising letters he had written Josie. They milked him for thousands of dollars, never returning the letters, until Fisk finally gave up and quit paying. Josie then filed suit against her former lover, and testimony at preliminary hearings threatened to bring into the open many of his and Gould's nefarious dealings on the stock market and in the business world. Stokes, however, was apparently unable to stand the publicity; just as the hearings reopened, on January 6, 1872, he caught Fisk

[15] Myers, *Great American Fortunes,* p. 493.

in Pike's Opera House in New York City and shot him. Fisk died within a few hours and Stokes later was tried and sentenced to four years in prison.

In spite of Jay Gould's disreputable methods, Gustavus Myers found a small saving grace for him in the fact that he was not "the politic sort of magnate who cut the pay of his workingmen and then as a solace presented them with a toy philanthropy; he did not polish greed with hypocrisy."[16]

Although it was missing from Gould's career, philanthropy was a characteristic and somewhat puzzling feature of the careers of many of his business contemporaries. Carnegie, Rockefeller, and others gave huge funds to churches and hospitals and endowed libraries, colleges, and foundations. What motivated them to do this? Was such behavior sheer hypocrisy, as Myers suggested, or was this aspect of American business ethics somehow rooted in the American cultural experience? Many historians believe that Puritan attitudes toward economic activity persisted and merged with Social Darwinism and other intellectual currents. For the Puritans, the accumulation of wealth had religious sanction; but once it was accumulated, the wealth was not to be squandered, because squandering had no religious sanction at all. The rich man was considered merely the manager of God's wealth; he was expected to use it for the enhancement of God's worldly kingdom.

Andrew Carnegie

The career of steel magnate Andrew Carnegie provides an excellent example of the way in which the Puritan doctrine of stewardship mingled with the newer ideas of Social Darwinism and laissez-faire capitalism. Andrew Carnegie was also, of course, the living proof of the American rags-to-riches story; as one historian put it, Carnegie mounted "the ladder of success so fast that he scorched the rungs."[17]

Carnegie's impoverished parents brought him to Amer-

[16] Ibid., p. 492.

[17] Bailey, *American Pageant,* p. 530.

ica from Scotland in 1848, and his first job was as a bobbin boy in a cotton factory. Later, as a messenger boy in a Pittsburgh telegraph office, the young Carnegie acquired such skill in operating the telegraph that he was made private secretary and personal telegrapher to Thomas Scott, an official of the Pennsylvania Railroad. Carnegie remained with the Pennsylvania for twelve years, advancing to superintendent of the Pittsburgh division. His most important achievement as a railroad man was his investment in the Woodruff Company, the original holder of the patents for Pullman sleeping cars; the profits from his investment represented Carnegie's first "strike" or accumulation of capital. In 1873, at the age of thirty-eight, he entered the business that became the foundation of America's industrial supremacy.

Andrew Carnegie.

Steel was not an important item in the America Carnegie had grown up in. It was simply too expensive to make. In the 1850's, however, a revolutionary steel fabricating procedure known as the Bessemer process had been invented in England. The Bessemer process made the production of cheap steel possible. Although coal for coking, iron ore, and other ingredients necessary for producing steel were abundant in the United States, no one had yet supplied the organizational genius, vision, energy, and capital to put all the pieces together on a large and profitable scale. Andrew Carnegie was foremost among those who supplied these missing elements.

Taking advantage of low construction costs attendant upon a severe depression during the years 1873 to 1875, Carnegie built a factory in Pittsburgh equipped to make steel by the Bessemer process. His choice of a location was a good one, for Pittsburgh was situated at the intersection of strategic transportation lines. Coal from the interior of Pennsylvania and iron ore from the rich Massabi region in Minnesota could be brought together there with a minimum of cost and Pittsburgh was indeed already an important ironmaking center.

Not satisfied with this advantage, Carnegie soon attempted to bring all of the elements of steel production under his company's control, thus insuring a dependable supply at stable prices. He secured control over key sources of coal and iron ore, over the production of coke for smelting, and over the operation of the necessary transportation facilities. As a result, by the end of the nineteenth century the Carnegie Steel Company was virtually self-sufficient.

American Antiquarian Society

The career of Andrew Carnegie was almost a Horatio Alger tale come true. Alger's enormously popular novels told of poor young men who gained fame and fortune through imagination, honest hard work, and more than a little luck.

Carnegie's company was a limited partnership rather than a corporation. Every share was held by someone who worked for the company, with Carnegie retaining a majority interest. This partnership ultimately involved about forty Pittsburgh millionaires, and Carnegie credited his success to the fact that he had surrounded himself with men of exceptional talent. When Carnegie sold out in 1901 to J. P. Morgan, his company became the basis for the U. S. Steel Corporation.

Andrew Carnegie was innovative. He did not hesitate to replace equipment made obsolete by new developments, and he hired chemists to find ways of making better steel. At the same time he was not above sharp practices. A ruthless competitor, he kept his prices low and in the process drove several steel companies out of business. He joined with other companies to fix prices, then violated the agreements by lowering his own prices. He kept his labor costs low, paying skilled workers ten to twelve dollars a week, barely enough to live on.

Like the Puritans, Carnegie perceived that the wealthy had a duty to society. As he himself said:

> This, then, is held to be the duty of the man of wealth: To set an example of modest, unostentatious living, shunning display or extravagance; to provide moderately for the legitimate wants of those dependent upon him; and, after doing so, to consider all surplus revenues which come to him simply as trust funds, which he is called upon to administer, and strictly bound as a matter of duty to administer in the manner which, in his judgment, is best calculated to produce the most beneficial results for the community—the man of wealth thus becoming the mere trustee and agent for his poorer brethren, bringing to their

> service his superior wisdom, experience, and ability to administer, doing for them better than they would or could do for themselves.[18]

Although he considered wealth a sacred trust in the hands of those most capable of serving the country, Carnegie's ideas were very similar to the views of William Graham Sumner and the Social Darwinists. He believed that one should be careful not to aid the unworthy and should avoid giving outright charity. The wealthy, he believed, should give their money to causes that did not encourage the survival of the unfit. His Social Darwinist attitudes were best reflected in this statement:

> Individualism will continue, but the millionaire will be but a trustee for the poor, intrusted for a season with a great part of the increased wealth of the community, but administering it for the community far better than it could or would have been done for itself. The best minds will thus have reached a stage in the development of the race in which it is clearly seen that there is no mode of disposing of surplus wealth creditable to thoughtful and earnest men into whose hands it flows, save by using it year by year for the general good.[19]

This drawing of Carnegie the philanthropic Scotsman appeared in the old *Life* magazine in 1905.

Culver Pictures

Building libraries squared with this philosophy, since they were not likely to perpetuate or encourage laziness or pauperism. And, although Carnegie contributed to a number of other philanthropic causes, his name is usually associated with the numerous libraries he established throughout the country. The satirist Finley Peter Dunne, in his *Dissertations by Mr. Dooley*, had this to say about Carnegie's idea of a worthy cause:

> No beggar is iver turned impty-handed fr'm th' dure. Th' pan-handler knocks and asts f'r a glass iv milk an' a roll.

[18] Andrew Carnegie, *The Gospel of Wealth and Other Timely Essays* (New York: Doubleday, Page & Co., 1906), p. 15.
[19] Ibid., pp. 18–19.

> "No sir," says Andhrew Carnaygie. "I will not pauperize this onworthy man. Nawthin' is worse f'r a beggar-man thin to make a pauper iv him. Yet it shall not be said iv me that I give nawthin to th' poor. Saunders, give him a libry . . . ."[20]

Despite his views on the natural superiority of the wealthy and his mistrust of the poor, Carnegie has been generally considered a humanitarian, ranking among the more constructive of nineteenth-century businessmen.

The Homestead Strike in Pennsylvania in 1892 blemished Carnegie's reputation. Up to that time his relations with workers in the steel industry had been good although somewhat paternalistic. He had professed to believe that trade unions were beneficial to both labor and capital and that the right of workingmen to combine was as sacred as the right of manufacturers to form associations. But, all of Carnegie's public statements notwithstanding, the Carnegie Company set out to destroy the Amalgamated Association of Iron and Steel Workers. During the Homestead Strike and its attendant violence and bloodshed, Carnegie was in Europe; one of his partners, Henry Clay Frick, acted on behalf of the company. Despite the fact that Frick used strong-armed and violent methods to crush the workers, methods which the philanthropic Carnegie could hardly approve of, the outcome of the struggle was enthusiastically accepted by the senior partner. Carnegie has, justifiably, been held responsible for Frick's actions and his reputation as a humanitarian has suffered accordingly.

John D. Rockefeller

If Carnegie was the leading "trustee" of the nation's wealth from steel, John D. Rockefeller held that distinction among those who made fortunes in the oil industry. The architect of the mammoth Standard Oil Company was just as interested in philanthropy as Carnegie. Rockefeller agreed with Carnegie's "Gospel of Wealth"—that it was the duty

[20] Quoted in Gail Kennedy, ed., *Democracy and the Gospel of Wealth* (Boston: D. C. Heath, 1949), p. 113.

of the rich to maintain their wealth and distribute it themselves. He defended this when he wrote:

> Up to the present time no scheme has yet presented itself which seems to afford a better method of handling capital than that of individual ownership. We might put our money into the Treasury of the Nation and of the various states, but we do not find any promise in the National or state legislatures . . . that the funds would be expounded for the general wealth more effectively than under the present methods, nor do we find in any schemes of socialism a promise that wealth would be more wisely administered for the general good.[21]

At first, the main source of requests for funds from Rockefeller was Baptist ministers and, for the most part, his donations went for religious and educational purposes. Rockefeller's choice of religion as a cause worthy of his philanthropy inspired a cartoon that appeared in a 1905 issue of *Colliers*, a muckraking magazine that made him a frequent target for its barbs. Rockefeller was shown in angelic garb with each hand holding a money bag representing his great oil fortune. The caption read:

Library of Congress

John D. Rockefeller.

> Praise John from whom oil blessings flow
> Praise him oil creatures here below.[22]

In 1913, Rockefeller's philanthropy was institutionalized with the chartering of the Rockefeller Foundation, established to support numerous worthy causes. This foundation, active since that time, has been especially generous in the fields of education and medical research, or in what Rockefeller termed "scientific giving."

[21] John D. Rockefeller, *Random Reminiscences of Men and Events* (New York: Doubleday, Doran & Co., 1933), pp. 159–160.

[22] Cartoon reprinted in Thomas A. Bailey, *The American Spirit: United States History as Seen by Contemporaries* (Lexington, Mass.: D. C. Heath, 1968), p. 522.

"With One Hand He Put a Penny in the Urn of Poverty and With the Other Took a Shilling Out"—a 1903 view of John D. Rockefeller's philanthropic activities.

Culver Pictures

Although Rockefeller's philanthropy was noteworthy as an expression of a certain aspect of the business ethics of his time, it was by no means the most characteristic feature of his career. Above all, Rockefeller symbolized monopoly. His ruthless elimination of competitors led critics of big business to draw many examples from his career to illustrate the evils of trusts.

Rockefeller was born in an upstate New York village in 1839. His father was a traveling salesman of quack medicine and it has been said that he made a practice of cheating his son in order to sharpen his wits. Rockefeller settled in Cleveland, where he went to work at a feed and coal store in 1855. Saving a large proportion of his earnings, which he invested in his own produce business, he quickly became a successful merchant. During the Civil War he invested in an oil refinery, and by 1865 he was devoting his full time to the oil business.

Because it cost little to make a start in the oil business, the industry was intensely competitive. As Rockefeller himself once put it, "all sorts of people . . . the butcher, the baker and the candlestick-maker, began to refine oil." Cleveland was an ideal location for oil refineries, a fact which Rockefeller was quick to realize. Both the Atlantic and Great Western and New York Central–Lake Shore railway lines passed through the city. This meant that the railroads had to compete with each other when they set rates for transporting crude oil from the fields in northwestern Pennsylvania and for carrying refined illuminating oil and kerosene to market. As a result, Cleveland refiners often paid less for long-distance transportation than their competitors. Railroads were inclined to try to make up for losses in competitive areas by setting exorbitantly high rates in areas where they faced no rivals, and refiners located in such areas were out of luck. Besides enjoying the advantage that accrued from rate competition between the railroads, Cleveland refiners could also ship to the Atlantic coast by way of the Great Lakes and the Erie Canal. Rockefeller's genius lay in recognizing that Cleveland could dominate the oil industry, even though the city might have disadvantages for other industries.

By the end of 1865, Rockefeller and his partners were operating the largest of Cleveland's thirty refineries. Although he borrowed heavilv for the purpose of expanding his operation, Rockefeller avoided any highly speculative or risky practices. Meticulously attentive to detail, he instituted a cost-accounting system that was accurate to the third decimal; stories have been told of how he carefully determined the exact number of drops of solder needed to seal an oil can, and then ordered that number to be used to save unnecessary expenditure. He also set out to develop a larger market for his products, sending his brother, whom he had taken in as a partner, to New York to secure the eastern and export trades.

The soundness of Rockefeller's operation enabled it to survive the depression that hit the oil industry in 1867–1868. In fact, Rockefeller used this occasion, as he did similar ones, to buy out small competitors who were on the brink of bankruptcy. Competition among the refiners who survived the depression entered a phase more savage than ever. Railroad rates and oil prices both were driven down to unprofitable levels. Rockefeller, through his new partner Henry M. Flagler, undertook to negotiate with the New York Central–Lake Shore Railroad system for very low special rates, in return for which the Rockefeller firm promised to forego all business with the competing line as well as all eastward shipments by water. Attracted by the lower unit cost of handling large-volume shipments and by the advantage of being able to count on regular shipments, the Lake Shore agreed to the offer. Rockefeller thus secured an inestimable advantage over his competitors. Meanwhile, he continued to reduce his costs through what is known as "vertical integration"—bringing as many of the elements of production under centralized control as possible. The firm began to make its own barrels, erecting a cooperage plant for that purpose. It built its own warehouses for storage. It started to manufacture its own sulfuric acid for refining and retained research chemists to improve refining methods. It developed and marketed all sorts of kerosene by-products, such as paraffin and machine lubricants, to bring about further savings. Eventually Rockefeller pushed vertical integration so far that his Standard Oil Company controlled almost every step from the procurement of crude oil to final product marketing.

In 1870, Rockefeller and his partners converted their firm into a joint stock company, the Standard Oil Company of Ohio, with Rockefeller as president and major stockholder. Two years later, the company became involved in one of the most brazen schemes of Rockefeller's career. Depression the previous year had hit the oil industry with crushing blows, leaving even large companies reeling and receptive to proposals for averting future uncertainties and disasters. In cooperation with the Erie, New York Central–Lake Shore, Michigan Southern, and Atlantic and Great Western railroads—virtually all the railroads that carried oil—the Pennsylvania Railroad formed the South Improvement Company together with the major oil refiners, the largest of which was Standard Oil. The railroads secretly agreed to raise their advertised rates drastically. The refiners who were members of the company agreed to divide their business among the railroads, an arrangement known as a pool. In return, they were to receive rebates, the difference between the advertised new rates and the original rates, and drawbacks, a portion of the increase their competitors outside the company would be paying. The object was to make it impossible for outsiders to compete with the members of the company, forcing them to sell out. News of this ingenious plan leaked out and destroyed it, but not before Rockefeller had persuaded numerous worried refiners to sell their companies to him at a fraction of their real value. Eventually angry crude-oil producers boycotted both the railroads and the refiners who were parties to the South Improvement Company. Then, responding to public pressure, the Pennsylvania legislature revoked the company's charter. The whole arrangement collapsed and competition continued to rage in the oil industry.

By the middle of the 1870's, Standard Oil Company had merged with most of the Cleveland refiners and with many concerns outside the city. It controlled more than half the refining industry and was pushing forward with more vertical integration. At this point the Pennsylvania Railroad, which had built its own refineries on the east coast under its subsidiary, the Empire Transportation Company, began to build pipelines aimed at low-cost, nonrailroad transportation of oil. This was a potential threat to Rockefeller. Enlisting the aid of the railroads who stood to lose business, he crushed the Empire Transportation Company and later bought its refinery, pipelines, tank cars, and collateral property. The surrender of many remaining independent refiners followed.

The final step in organizing the oil monopoly came when the Standard Oil trust was born. An Ohio corporation, Standard Oil was prohibited by state law from owning plants in other states or from owning stock in out-of-state corporations. The need to integrate the management of various Rockefeller properties throughout the country with Standard Oil of Ohio ran contrary to this statute. To escape the dilemma, Rockefeller and his associates created a board of nine trustees, and gave this board or trust general supervisory powers over all the subsidiary and allied companies of Standard Oil as well as over the parent company itself. The trust owned stock in the separate companies and its stockholders received trust certificates on which they were paid dividends from the various companies jointly managed by the nine trustees. This legal device made it possible to vertically integrate all the various steps to marketing without the need to secure new company charters.

The profits from the Standard Oil Company placed Rockefeller among America's richest men. By 1892 he was worth over $800 million and his influence extended to virtually every area of the economy. As a contemporary business expert observed:

> These men . . . either entirely control or make their influence felt to a marked degree in all the Greater Trusts. They are in fact the real fathers of the Trust idea in this country, and, of course, have always been the controlling factors in that most far-reaching and successful of all Trusts, the Standard Oil Company. This latter corporation, with a par value capitalization of $97,500,000, absolutely dominates the oil industry of the United States, supplying

> 84% of the domestic demand of oil, and over 90% of the export demand.[23]

Rockefeller's power lay not only in oil. Rockefeller interests controlled copper and smelter industries and were influential in such other areas as tobacco, steel, public services and utilities, railroads, and banking institutions. To some Americans, Rockefeller appeared to be a dangerous autocrat.

In 1904 Ida M. Tarbell published her *History of the Standard Oil Company.* She was extremely critical of Rockefeller's motives, ethics, and especially his power:

> As a natural result of these extraordinary powers, we see, as in the case of Standard Oil Company, the price of a necessity of life within the control of a group of nine men, as able, as energetic, and as ruthless in business operations as any nine men the world has ever seen combined. They have exercised their power over prices with almost preternatural skill. It has been their most cruel weapon in stifling competition, a sure means of reaping usurious dividends, and, at the same time, a most persuasive argument in hoodwinking the public.[24]

Rockefeller regarded this as unfounded, unfair criticism and he defended his kind of corporation as a necessity in the modern business world. He argued that the capital for industrial progress could be raised only through such an operation. Not only did Rockefeller consider corporations themselves to be necessities but he also believed that they provided great advantages and were generally a positive good. "It is . . . true that combinations of capital are bound to grow," he said,

> and this need not alarm even the most timid if the corporation . . . is properly conducted with the one regard for the rights of others. The day of individual competition in

[23] John Moody, *The Truth About Trusts* (New York: Moody Publishing Co., 1904), p. 490.

[24] Ida Tarbell, *The History of the Standard Oil Company* (New York: Macmillan Co., 1925), p. 230.

> large affairs is past and gone—you might just as well argue that we should go back to hand labour and throw away our efficient machines—and the sober good sense of the people will accept this fact when they have studied and tried it out. Just see how the list of stockholders in the great corporations is increasing by leaps and bounds. This means that all these people are becoming partners in great business. It is a good thing—it will bring a feeling of increased responsibility to the managers of the corporations and will make the people who have their interests involved study the facts impartially before condemning or attacking them.[25]

Rockefeller did not deny that Standard Oil destroyed competition. But according to him, competition unnecessarily wasted energy and resources. There was a need for men to open new fields and develop new industries. There was no need for men to enter existing fields and compete where an industry was being managed efficiently. Standard Oil had been built by hard work and sound business management. The real reason that little competition existed, said Rockefeller, was that Standard Oil sold its products cheaply and other, less efficient companies could not compete. Rockefeller had entered a very shaky industry; he believed that he had made it a model of stability and efficiency.

Responding to Rockefeller's claim that Standard Oil's great efficiency had lowered prices, critics argued that most of these reductions had been caused by increasing efficiency in production and transportation throughout the whole industry and not through any actions taken solely by Standard Oil. They also pointed out that Standard Oil lowered prices when it wished to ruin a competitor. Afterward prices returned to previous levels and in some instances went a little higher. Ida Tarbell especially questioned Rockefeller's claims:

> To believe that the Standard Oil Combination, or any other similar aggregation, would lower prices except under

[25] Rockefeller, *Random Reminiscences,* pp. 65–66.

> the pressure of the competition they were trying to kill, argues an amazing gullibility. Human experience long ago taught us that if we allowed a man or a group of men autocratic powers in government or church, they used that power to oppress and defraud the public.[26]

Tarbell believed that Rockefeller and other industrialists had gained a despotic power in commerce that was just as dangerous to freedom and justice as any other form of despotism.

John Pierpont Morgan

In spite of the overwhelming power Rockefeller came to exercise over the American economy, it never equaled the power eventually attained by the greatest giant of the age—John Pierpont Morgan. Unlike Gould, Carnegie, and Rockefeller, Morgan did not rise from humble origins. He was the son of the prominent international banker, Junius Spencer Morgan; the family wealth had originated even earlier with J. P. Morgan's grandfather. In 1856, J. P. Morgan joined his father in the family firm and began a career that was to make the House of Morgan one of the most powerful banking institutions in the world, and Morgan himself the most extraordinary financier of them all.

Perhaps because Morgan did not need to resort to ruthless tactics to acquire his initial wealth, he was never subjected to the kind of criticism that was heaped on Jay Gould or to the rumors of "tainted wealth" that Rockefeller encountered throughout his career. His abilities were considered the highest in the financial world, and historians have generally praised his role in helping to organize American industry on an efficient—even though monopolistic—basis.

In this respect, Morgan's first major contribution was to help reorganize many of the country's railroads. He used his international banking house to generate capital for the merging of railroad lines that had been weakened or bankrupted by reckless and unscrupulous promoters or by

[26] Tarbell, *History of Standard Oil*, p. 229.

simple-minded mismanagement. In each merger or consolidation, people friendly to Morgan were placed in control of the reorganized railroad by means of a "voting trust" that gave his associates all the voting power of the stock. By the end of the nineteenth century, only the E. H. Harriman and the Gould railroad systems remained entirely independent of Morgan's financial control.

The banking house of Morgan proved indispensable in mobilizing the capital necessary to finance the consolidation of many other industries as well. Its most spectacular operation came in 1901 with the formation of the largest corporation in the world. Financing the merger of his own steel companies with those of Andrew Carnegie, William H. Moore, John W. Gates, and John D. Rockefeller, Morgan created the U. S. Steel Corporation and virtually selected the directors himself.

In a similar manner, Morgan extended his control over such a wide variety of industries that he became the supreme symbol of financial power in America. Altogether, eleven Morgan partners held seventy-two directorships in forty-seven of the largest corporations in the country. In addition to railroad interests and U. S. Steel, Morgan came to dominate International Harvester, General Electric, and American Telephone and Telegraph. His power touched every conceivable aspect of the American economy, as a contemporary observer affirmed:

> The great Morgan enterprises in the industrial world are the Steel and Shipping Trusts, the Electrical Supply Trust, the Rubber Trust, and a score or more of smaller aggregations. In the public utility field the Morgan interests dominate a series of lesser enterprises, but have never been so conspicuous in these lines as have the Rockefeller financiers.
>
> But it is in the railroad world that the Morgan influence makes its greatest claim for public attention. . . . The Morgan group of steam railroad properties embraces over 47,000 miles of lines, or nearly twice the mileage of any other one group; and its capitalization exceeds $2,265,000,000, a sum far in excess of that of any of the other five

> groups, and, in fact, amounting to nearly 25% of all the group railroad capital of the United States. . . . Another feature about the Morgan group is that in most cases the lines embraced absolutely dominate certain sections of the country; such as, for instance, the entire South and the Great Northwest.
>
> The Morgan domination . . . makes itself felt through the means and influence of large metropolitan financial institutions and great banks, such as the National Bank of Commerce, First National Bank, Chase National Bank, and Liberty National Bank. The great life insurance companies, such as the Mercantile, Guaranty and Central Trust, are generally rated as being at least partially under the Morgan control.[27]

The extent of Morgan's power was illustrated dramatically in 1895 when the United States government faced a serious financial crisis. In 1894, for the first time since the Civil War, government expenditures had exceeded revenues —by $61 million. The Treasury's supply of gold was at a dangerously low level and President Grover Cleveland decided to seek the aid of international bankers. A syndicate composed of J. P. Morgan and Company, August Belmont and Company, and several powerful national banks, was organized to furnish the government with some $62 million in gold. One of Morgan's contemporaries on Wall Street described the syndicate's terms for this service:

> Their terms as now submitted, in the crisis of January 1895, were extremely harsh; they measured with little mercy the emergency of the Treasury. They unfolded what they believed to be a practicable plan for both restoring and maintaining the Treasury reserve, but they made the consideration for their services the allotment of a thirty-year four per cent bond at a price equivalent to 104½, when the existing United States four per cents, with less than half as long to run, were bringing 111 on the market. This was asking a heavy concession; no such demand has been

[27] Moody, *The Truth About Trusts,* p. 492.

made by any Government-bond syndicate during the present generation.[28]

Although many people considered the terms harsh, Morgan was credited with extending a patriotic hand to the United States Treasury in a time of crisis. The syndicate's operation was extremely profitable, since the Morgan group immediately sold the bonds to investors at prices substantially higher than they had paid the government. Criticism was not absent, however, and some people accused President Cleveland of openly selling out the people of the United States to the Morgan syndicate. Whatever interpretation was placed on this transaction, one point was abundantly clear—John Pierpont Morgan was power personified. When a president of the United States felt forced to seek the aid of a group of international bankers in order to preserve the financial integrity of the nation, nothing more needs to be said about banking power of the time.

Morgan's reputation reached its height in the aftermath of the Panic of 1907, and for his role in that crisis the press hailed him as the "Savior of the Nation." *Pearson's Magazine*, which carried an article entitled "Morgan the Magnificent," was typical. No less a figure than John D. Rockefeller wrote in praise of Morgan:

> Since 1857 I can remember all the great panics, but I believe the panic of 1907 was the most trying. No one escaped from it, great or small. Important institutions had to be supported and carried through the time of distrust and unreasoning fear. To Mr. Morgan's real and effective help I should join with other business men and give great praise. His commanding personality served a most valuable end. He acted quickly and resolutely when quickness and decision were the things most needed to regain confidence, and he was efficiently seconded by many able and leading financiers of the country who cooperated courageously and effectively to restore confidence and prosperity.[29]

[28] Alexander Dana Noyes, *Forty Years of American Finance* (New York: G. P. Putnam's Sons, 1909), pp. 234–235.

[29] Rockefeller, *Random Reminiscences*, pp. 134–135.

Brown Brothers

J. P. Morgan loved art nearly as much as he loved power. He spent most of his great fortune on paintings and rare books.

In 1907 a group of speculators tried and failed to corner the stock of United Copper Company, losing considerable money in the process. One of them, F. Augustus Heinze, was the head of the Mercantile National Bank and there were rumors that bank funds were involved in the speculation. A run began on the Mercantile bank, and, as rumor fed on rumor, other banks were soon beseiged by depositors seeking to withdraw their money; the panic spread across the country. Some banks, unable to meet the sudden demand, failed.

The whole financial community looked to Morgan for leadership in the crisis and he provided it, if for no other reason than that continued panic could endanger even his powerful institutions. He placed funds from his own bank at the disposal of a number of threatened banks and persuaded the heads of financial institutions to cooperate to help each other weather the storm. The panic was halted, although many months passed before the financial markets of the country returned to normal.

Morgan, at least in his younger years, was not above dealing in a somewhat shady fashion. In 1863 he and an associate quietly bought up gold, although not with the grand plan of cornering the market as Jay Gould later tried to do. Making sure the news got out, the two speculators shipped half their holdings abroad, driving up the price of the other half and effectively devaluating the national currency at a time when the country was in trouble. Morgan and his partner profited handsomely. Two years earlier Morgan had lent a Simon Stevens $20,000 to purchase outmoded rifles, which Stevens in turn sold to General John C. Frémont for the War Department. The rifles—many of them defective—became security for the loan and passed from Morgan's possession to the government, which paid Morgan for them directly. It has never been determined whether or not Morgan actually knew that Stevens was engaged in fraud; congressional investigators concluded that he was simply a middleman and placed no blame on him. Morgan's successful speculation in gold was undoubtedly legitimate but it could hardly be called patriotic. His involvement in the rifle scandal apparently was only peripheral. Neither incident, however, added luster to his reputation and both became ammunition in the hands of hostile writers later on.

On the whole, Morgan has received a better press than some of his contemporaries like John D. Rockefeller and Jay Gould. Yet he did not escape criticism from reformers concerned over the concentration of such enormous power in the hands of one individual, nor has he been without detractors among historians. Whether one regards Morgan and others as robber barons or industrial statesmen depends, of course, on one's point of view, although it is possible with respect to many of them to strike a balance. Rockefeller increased the efficiency of oil production and distribution. He also ruthlessly crushed competition. Morgan did much to bring European capital to the United States and he was instrumental in bailing out the federal government in a time of financial crisis. None of his services, however, even in a time of national crisis, were free; he made enormous amounts of money on them. Jay Gould may have been the greatest scoundrel of his age, yet even Gustavus Myers found him no worse than many of his more pious—and hypocritical—business associates. Gould proclamied no theories, nor did he ever suggest that anything he did was for anybody's good but his own. And perhaps the fact that his were among the few western railroads that remained free of Morgan's control kept rail transportation at least to some extent competitive. What can be said about these men without much fear of contradiction is that they truly represented their age and symbolized all that was good and bad about it.

SUGGESTED READINGS

Adams, Charles Francis. *Chapters of Erie*. Cornell University Press.

Allen, Frederick Lewis. *The Great Pierpont Morgan*. Harper & Row, Perennial Library.

Allen, Frederick Lewis. *Lords of Creation*. Quadrangle.

Carnegie, Andrew. *The Gospel of Wealth and Other Timely Essays*. Harvard University Press, Belknap Press.

Degler, Carl. *Out of the Past: The Forces That Shaped Modern America*. Harper & Row, Colophon Books.

Drew, Daniel. *The Book of Daniel Drew*. Frontier Press Co.

Hacker, Louis M. *American Capitalism: Its Promise and Accomplishment*. Van Nostrand, Anvil Books.

Josephson, Matthew. *The Robber Barons*. Harcourt Brace Jovanovich, Harvest Books.

Kennedy, Gail, ed. *Democracy and the Gospel of Wealth*. D. C. Heath.

Tarbell, Ida. *The History of Standard Oil Company*. Edited by D. M. Chalmers. W. W. Norton.

Library of Congress

"Harvesting on a Bonanza Farm," 1891. "Bonanza farms" were large landholdings on the Great Plains, where a farmer using mechanized equipment could grow acres upon acres of a single crop like wheat. The result was often a "mine of wealth." But few farmers could afford to operate on this scale without going into debt, and farmers large and small were at the mercy of the weather, unpredictable farm prices, and monopolies which controlled the goods and services they had to buy.

THE FARMERS

During the years following the Civil War, American agriculture underwent a revolution brought about by the expansion of farm land, the application of science and machinery to farming processes, and the use of modern transportation to carry farm products to a worldwide market. "This revolution," Samuel Eliot Morison and Henry Steele Commager have written,

> meant a shift from husbandry to machine-farming, and from subsistence to commercial farming; made agriculture an intimate though subordinate part of the industrial system; exposed the farmer to the viscissitudes of the industrial economy and the world market; and did not always bring comparable returns.[1]

Agricultural machinery, with the notable exception of the cotton gin and to some extent the reaper, had been relatively unimportant before 1860. The Civil War generated a great demand for increased food production and for labor-saving devices to replace farm workers siphoned off by the army. The manufacture and use of agricultural machinery expanded rapidly. While perhaps 100,000 reapers were in operation in 1861, during the war years the number increased dramatically to over 225,000. After the war the market was flooded with new inventions, and by the 1890's an enormous transformation of traditional agri-

[1] Samuel Eliot Morison and Henry Steele Commager, *The Growth of the American Republic*, 2 vols. (New York: Oxford University Press, 1962), 2: 78.

culture had occurred. The Oliver chilled-steel plow enabled farmers to cut through the deep and tangled roots of prairie grass, opening much rich, black soil to planting. George Appleby's twine binder, a device that eliminated the time-consuming task of binding sheaves of grain by hand, went on the market in 1878 and underwent constant change and improvement. During the 1870's innumerable other machines appeared or were greatly improved, among them the steam threshing machine, the mowing machine, the four-plow cultivator, the potato planter, the manure spreader, the poultry incubator, the mechanical hay drier, the cream separator, the corn planter, and the corn binder, husker, and sheller. Morison and Commager underscored the significance of these developments with the following statistics:

> In 1830 it required something over half an hour to prepare the ground and sow one bushel of wheat; in 1900 two minutes sufficed for this operation. With the hand cradle of 1830 a man could harvest 20 bushels of grain in 61 hours; by 1900 he could perform the same work in less than three hours. It took 21 hours to harvest a ton of timothy hay in 1850; half a century later, four hours. It was this vast saving in labor which made it possible for a proportionately smaller number of farmers to feed an ever-increasing number of city-dwellers and have a surplus left over for export.[2]

The production of farm machinery became a huge and powerful industry and, as in other industries, monopolies developed. The greatest of these combinations began with the reaper and Cyrus McCormick.

Cyrus H. McCormick.

International Harvester Company

Cyrus Hall McCormick

Born on a farm in Rockbridge County, Virginia, on February 15, 1809, McCormick had little formal education. Not until he was twenty-two did he exhibit any inventive ability; in 1831, however, he developed and applied for a patent on a hillside plow. While working on this invention he had

[2] Ibid., p. 285.

also labored over the development of a device his father had attempted to perfect but had abandoned, a mechanical reaper. The reaper McCormick finally tested in 1831 was not entirely satisfactory, but it did contain seven essential elements that would ensure its ultimate success. According to McCormick's grandson these were:

> The straight reciprocating knife, whereby the standing grain would be attacked by lateral motion as well as by the forward movement of the machine. (This the inventor himself regarded as the most vital of the elements.)
>
> The fingers or guards for the knife, which supported the grain at the moment of cutting.
>
> The reel, which gathered the grain in front of the reaper and held the heads in place as the fingers held the stalks.
>
> The platform, on which the severed grain might fall to be raked away in a swath.
>
> The main wheel, directly behind the horse, which carried the machine and operated gears to actuate the moving parts.
>
> The principle of cutting to one side of the line of draft, which permitted the horse to walk on the stubble while the cutter bar worked in the standing grain.
>
> The divider at the outer end of the cutter bar, to divide the standing grain from that which was to be reaped.[3]

McCormick had no immediate plans for the mass production and sale of his device, preferring first to make improvements. The results of an initial policy error caused him to change his mind, however, and led to the concentration of production in one city. "McCormick's mistake," wrote Roger Burlingame,

> —and it is important to our story because it shows the early need for concentration and a kind of "dictatorship" in mass-production industry—was in licensing various manufacturers to build his reapers instead of supervising the manufacture himself. He did this in western New York, in Ohio, in Missouri and in Illinois. The result was the direct

[3] Cyrus McCormick, *The Century of the Reaper* (Boston: Houghton Mifflin, 1931), pp. 17–18.

> opposite of mass production. (This can be done more easily today when machinery, patterns, specification sheets, materials and so on are standardized.) Every licensed manufacturer turned out a different reaper. Each incorporated ideas of his own and turned out what he thought was a prettier or more efficient job. From the customers came a variety of protests. The reapers were not as represented, not as advertised, not as promised. McCormick checked as quickly as he could and his discovery that the complaints were all too true led him to the great decision of his life. . . .

McCormick decided to locate his factory in Chicago, which, because of its central location and the plains and prairies that lay beyond it, was an extremely farsighted choice. At this time Chicago was little more than a small town on the expanding frontier, but a railroad was already building toward the Mississippi River and the lake port was developing rapidly. McCormick's industry would expand with the city.

Cyrus McCormick himself moved to Chicago in the spring of 1847. Within four years, according to his own estimate, he had sold a thousand reapers. By 1860 the McCormick Reaper Works was producing 4,000 machines annually. Although the Chicago fire of 1871 destroyed company buildings, valuable patterns, and the entire output of machines for the next year's harvest, McCormick recovered quickly. Three years later his factory was turning out 12,000 reapers a year. Output continued to climb throughout the remainder of the century, and by 1901 capacity had reached 1,400 agricultural machines of various kinds for every working day of ten hours. At the busiest season, McCormick employed 7,000 persons to manufacture harvesters, mowers, rakers, tedders (hay spreaders), and other farm implements.

The reaper was McCormick's only invention and technical contribution. After moving to Chicago he concentrated on the details of running an ever-expanding business, de-

[4] Roger Burlingame, *Machines That Built America* (New York: Harcourt, Brace, 1953), p. 93.

pending on others for innovations and improvements in products. "Because the name McCormick has become so celebrated in connection with agricultural machinery," wrote Burlingame,

> many believe that he invented the improvements which made the reaper into a harvester. This was not, however, true. None of them were his. By the time he reached Chicago, Cyrus McCormick had ceased to be an inventor. From then on he was a manufacturer of his own and other men's inventions. Through years of cutthroat competition he managed to absorb most of these. The beautiful device which bound a sheaf of grain with twine and cast it aside—a completely automatic performance—was invented not by McCormick but by Charles Withington; yet the machine became a McCormick product. Other manufacturers, however, continued to offer dangerous rivalry until, at last, at the turn of the century the survivors formed the International Harvester Corporation which has dominated the field ever since.[5]

The formation of International Harvester in 1902—under the auspices and guidance of the House of Morgan—was in tune with the times. Mergers had become common. They were designed, on the one hand, to tidy up the competitive situation—as John D. Rockefeller had done in oil—and on the other, as those who engineered these mergers insisted, to give the customer a more reliable product and better service. Cyrus McCormick's grandson explained:

> There can be no question but that self-preservation lay uppermost in the minds of the company presidents who sat around that table. The evils of the harvester war were fresh in their troubled minds. But there were many other cogent reasons why the International Harvester Company should be formed. The competitive methods of the Nineties were not only murderous, but wasteful in the extreme and detrimental to retail agent and consumer as well as to manufacturer. Farmers had bought enormous quantities of harvesting machinery in 1902 from the five organizations,

[5] Ibid., pp. 98–99.

> more than they really needed. The pressure of salesmanship was such that the harvester companies were forcing more implements on the public than it had any occasion to buy. A machine which might have lasted for nearly ten years was declared obsolete in less than five; and the farmer's bill for new equipment was beyond all reason—not because of the price per unit, which was ruinously low, but because of the many units needlessly sold. The local dealers were crippled by their own numbers. Competition had decreed that all over the United States, in every town, at every crossroads, there must be a McCormick or a Deering dealer. The three other companies were less widely represented; but they, too, had flung as far as possible the array of their distributors. More than forty thousand dealers across the land were far too many. None of them could grow, none could become prosperous, none could do more than imitate in his own neighborhood the feud methods of the big companies. They fought, too, and their fall was even more rapid.[6]

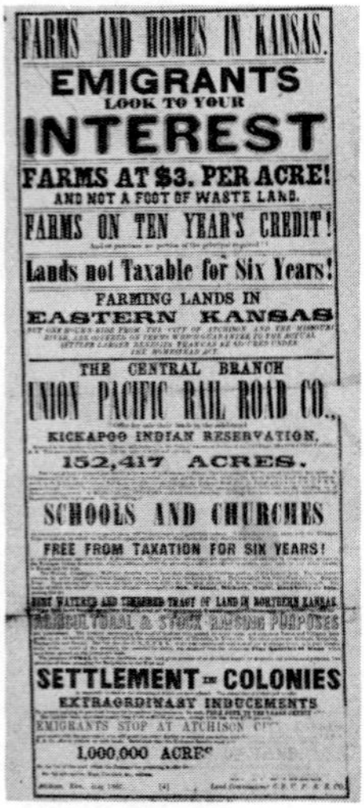

Advertisements like this one, which appeared in an Atchison, Kansas, newspaper in 1867, attracted many would-be farmers to the Great Plains states.

Baker Library, Harvard University

To merge, then, and form a mighty combination was only a sensible, intelligent thing to do.

Farmers and Reformers

In the meantime, although farmers enjoyed the labor-saving benefits of machines, they were otherwise far from happy with their lot. On the whole, farming had ceased to be an independent, largely self-sufficient, family operation. Farmers had become intricately interwoven in a worldwide economy, dependent on a distant market and on long-distance transportation facilities. As the nineteenth century progressed, agricultural prices—except during the Civil War—fell more than those of other goods, many of which were held up by monopolistic practices in industry. A bushel of wheat bought a farmer less and less. Few, if any, of the gains from improved transportation and produce-handling facilities were passed on to farmers. Railroad and grain elevator operators simply soaked the captive rustics

[6] McCormick, *Century of the Reaper*, pp. 114–115.

for all the traffic would bear. In addition, whether it was true or not, farmers firmly believed that banks and mortgage companies took advantage of them with usurious rates of interest—and as seasonal producers or as entrepreneurs wishing to expand, farmers had frequent need for loans. During deflationary times—during the hair-raising depressions of the 1870's and 1890's, for example—farmers had to repay the loans they had accumulated during inflationary times with dollars now worth more than the dollars they had borrowed when the economy was in a boom period. Since the major money power lay in the East—in financial institutions like the House of Morgan—discontent with loans and interest rates tended to generate regional as well as class complaints. As Morison and Commager have pointed out,

> Some states attempted, through usury laws, to fix low interest rates, but such laws were flouted or evaded, and interest rates in the farm belts of the South and the West were seldom below 10 per cent and in the 'nineties much higher. Inadequate banking facilities were in part re-

Culver Pictures

In this 1888 cartoon, the farmer is an unwelcome guest—"the political poor relation"—at a banquet of monopolists who are eating "trust roast" from the "congressional kitchen" and listening to a "high tariff symphony."

> sponsible for this situation. In 1880, for example, the per capita banking power of the Eastern states was $176, of the Central states $27, and of the Southern states $10. Furthermore, with the rise in the value of money after the Civil War, the farmers' debt appreciated steadily. It took approximately 1200 bushels of wheat, corn, oats, barley, and rye to buy a $1000 mortgage in the years 1867 to 1869; between 1886 and 1888 it took approximately 2300 bushels of the same crops to repay that mortgage.[7]

Farmers were frequently at the mercy of moneylenders, grain elevator operators, and railroad companies. (In good times, farmers, like other businessmen, borrowed optimistically—in order to expand their operations; they were however sometimes caught short by bad times, and so it was not entirely fair for farmers to blame the bankers for the consequences of their own desire to increase their holdings or production.) Essentially, however, farmers were enmeshed in an economic and climatic web. Much of their produce—wheat and corn, for example—was sold in a worldwide market. Bumper crops in Canada, Argentina, or Australia drove prices down, and worldwide prices affected those on the domestic market. A period of poor crops in the United States did not always bring higher prices; if weather had been more favorable in another part of the world, world supplies might be diminished only slightly. Farmers could control neither the market nor the weather—and many years would pass before anyone seriously suggested that farmers form broad cooperative marketing organizations or that they deliberately cut back their production to keep prices high.

Farmers sold in a competitive market. They bought machinery and other goods in a market that, thanks to trusts and monopolies and tariffs, was not nearly so open. Farm machinery companies, fertilizer producers, furniture and clothing firms, and others from whom farmers bought could control their prices much more easily than the farmers could. And while American farmers had to compete with

[7] Morison and Commager, *Growth*, 2: 298.

Argentine and Australian wheat on the world market and have their incomes influenced by foreign production, American manufacturers, sheltered by high protective tariffs, competed practically not at all with foreign producers on the home market.

To the farmers, perhaps in part because they were reminded of them so often, the railroads were the principal villains, the major cause of their misery. Railroads were completely unregulated by state or federal governments until late in the nineteenth century. They set their own rates, frequently by agreement among themselves. Small farmers were discriminated against in favor of large shippers. Railroads awarded special low rates to long-distance shippers and made up for it by raising rates to farmers using short hauls. Since the richest farmers were not short-haulers, this rate discrimination hastened the decline of the small farmer, a decline that rich farmers were not particularly upset about. Elevator owners and millers probably ranked second on the farmers' list of evil-doers, while moneylenders floated up and down in favor depending on the times and the need for loans.

Farmers were not entirely overlooked by reformers worried about the growth of monopolies and the deteriorating influence of industrialization on the quality of American life. Generally, however, critics of the social and economic system concentrated on urban problems, giving farmers and their troubles an occasional sympathetic but passing glance. Washington Gladden's comment in 1890 was typical of the vague, emotional way in which reformers tended to recognize the farmers' problems:

> The farmers of the United States are up in arms. They are the bone and sinew of the nation; they produce the largest share of its wealth; but they are getting, they say, the smallest share for themselves. The American farmer is steadily losing ground. His burdens are heavier every year and his gains are more meager; he is beginning to fear that he may be sinking into a servile condition. He has waited long for the redress of his grievances; he proposes to wait no longer. Whatever he can do by social combinations,

> or by united political action, to remove the disabilities under which he is suffering, he intends to do at once and with all his might. There is no doubt at all that the farmers of this country are tremendously in earnest just now, and they have reason to be. Beyond question they are suffering sorely. The business of farming has become, for some reasons, extremely unprofitable. With the hardest work and with the sharpest economy, the average farmer is unable to make both ends meet; every year closes with debt, and the mortgage grows till it devours the land.[8]

For the most part farmers relied on their own kind to define their problems a little more specifically and to develop concrete solutions for them.

The Grange

The National Grange of the Patrons of Husbandry—the Grange—was founded in 1867 as a means to provide social and educational activities for isolated, lonely farm families. By 1874 membership had reached 1.5 million in 20,000 local chapters, many of which, by then, had turned into arenas for the discussion of economic and political problems. With Grange support, reform candidates were elected to legislatures in Kansas, Illinois, and Washington in 1874, and during the 1870's Wisconsin had a Granger governor. Granger legislators enacted laws to regulate railroad rates and make them uniform for all shippers, a signal victory over the "steel octopus" which had recently extended its reach to the western plains. Railroad companies eventually appealed these Granger-sponsored state laws to the United States Supreme Court, which declared them unconstitutional because only the federal government could regulate interstate trade. Later, farmer pressure helped bring about the Interstate Commerce Act of 1887, a beginning, however small, of federal railroad regulation.

Ignatius Donnelly.

Culver Pictures

One of the most persuasive spokesmen for the Granger movement was Ignatius Donnelly. As a Republican, Donnelly had been lieutenant governor of Minnesota and a

[8] Washington Gladden, "The Embattled Farmers," *The Forum* 10 (November 1890): 315.

member of the U.S. House of Representatives; he left the Republican party when he became convinced that it was committed to the interests of the wealthy. He was active in organizing local Grange chapters, and from 1874 to 1879 he edited a periodical called *The Anti-Monopolist.* In a speech in 1873, Donnelly summed up the farmers' railroad dilemma:

> The railroad men are sharp, quick, and bold. The farmers are dull, and slow, and timid. The railroads are thoroughly organized and act together. The farmers have not heretofore been organized, and have divided on a dozen immaterial questions. The railroads buy up the politicians, and the politicians humbug the farmers. The railroads act for themselves; the farmers dare do nothing without consulting some lawyer, editor, or cross-roads wire-puller. The railroads own the newspapers, and the newspapers lash the farmers back into party lines. In short, the corporations are superb rogues, and the farmers are helpless and honest fools. If any man takes the farmer's part, editors, politicians and corporations raise a howl, a regular hue and cry against him, and too often the very farmers drop their hoes and scythes and join with a yell in the pursuit. If any man takes the corporation's part there is no hue and cry; they measure him by his capacity for service, and pay him accordingly.[9]

An outdoors Granger meeting, with a speaker telling farmers to fight for their rights.

The Greenback Movement

Agrarian interests found an outlet in the Greenback movement in the 1870's; they were joined by labor in the formation of the Greenback-Labor party, a group that enjoyed some success. At the height of its power in 1878, this party polled over one million votes and elected fourteen candidates to Congress, among them Ignatius Donnelly.

Greenbackers advocated lower tariffs on manufactured goods and they argued for the enactment of personal and corporate income taxes. Their main concern, however, was with paper money, and not with its quality but its quantity.

To help finance the Civil War, the federal government had issued millions of dollars worth of paper money that

[9] Ignatius Donnelly, *Donnelliana*, p. 136.

was not backed by gold, and at the war's end about $400 million worth of this paper was in circulation. During the war, the government had borrowed money by issuing bonds, most of which had been purchased with greenbacks that had gradually depreciated in value. At the war's end, the question then arose whether the government should pay off these bonds in greenbacks or in specie—gold. Farmers and workingmen preferred redemption in greenbacks; many bondholders and businessmen favored redemption at face value in gold, which would make the bonds more profitable items. A related question concerned government policy toward currency supply generally: should the government allow paper currency that was not backed by gold to remain in circulation, or should it return to the prewar practice of exchanging paper currency for gold upon demand? The gold value of greenbacks fluctuated almost from month to month—sometimes falling to a low of about fifty cents' worth to the dollar, sometimes rising to nearly eighty cents' worth—and as a result greenbacks were items for speculation. (Their speculatory aspect, incidentally, was involved in Jay Gould and Jim Fisk's attempt to corner the gold market in 1869, an incident which is discussed in Chapter Two.) Greenback inflation, however, had made credit easier and money cheaper; farmers and workingmen wanted more of it. They preferred an abundance of unstable currency to a tight supply of specie.

The nation fell into financial panic and depression in 1873, at a time when about $382 million worth of greenbacks were in circulation. Seeking to prime the economic pump a little, Congress in 1874 passed a bill to increase the supply to $400 million, obviously an inflationary measure. President Ulysses S. Grant vetoed the bill. The following year, Congress passed a resumption act which restored gold payment for both greenbacks and bonds, and President Grant signed it. The Resumption Act of 1875 *threatened* to remove greenback currency from circulation; the threat was enough, and most people turned their greenbacks in for gold, which they tended to spend less freely than paper currency. This meant that the total amount of money in circulation also decreased, and so there was less money available to farmers for loans. Farmers and labor groups thus lost their fight for inflation and easy money. In 1876, the Greenback-Labor party ran Peter Cooper for president. Cooper polled only 81,000 votes, but two years later the party had much greater success in congressional elections—nearly 1,000,000 votes.

Contrary to predictions, the anti-inflationary Resumption Act of 1875 did not lead to the wholesale impoverishment of farmers and working people. By 1880, the Greenback movement was on the decline, even though James B. Weaver, a former Union general and war hero, received a little over 300,000 votes as Greenback-Labor candidate for president that year.

James B. Weaver and the Populist Party

James B. Weaver remained active in politics after 1880, gaining a seat in Congress as a representative from Iowa in 1884 and retaining it in 1886. He did not stop talking about the money question that had placed him on the national stage as a presidential candidate in 1880. "Our national banking system is the result of a compact between Congress and certain speculative syndicates," he alleged in a magazine article in 1892,

> Congress agreeing to exercise the power to create money, to bestow it as a gift, and to enforce its circulation; while the syndicates are to determine the quantity, and say when it shall be issued and retired. . . . It is a fine exhibition of Democratic government to see our Treasury Department create the currency, bestow it as a gift upon money lenders, and then stand by with cruel indifference and witness the misfortunes, the sharp competition, and the afflictions of life drive the rest of its devoted subjects to the feet of these purse-proud barons as supplicants and beggars for extortionist, second-hand favors.[10]

The late 1880's brought even more serious problems to farmers of the plains—terrible drought and the end of a land boom that had begun during the preceding decade. A

[10] James B. Weaver, "The Threefold Contention of Industry," *The Arena* 5 (March 1892): 433–434.

great deal of virgin soil—much of it not suited for farming—had been plowed, many small, agrarian towns had sprung up, and land speculation had run wild in parts of Kansas, Nebraska, and the Dakotas. Most of the new farms were heavily mortgaged to eastern bankers, and all this was of course the farmers' doing. Rain had been plentiful for several years. Then in 1887 it practically ceased to fall. The drought continued into the 1890's, turning prairie soil to dust and hopes to ashes. Between 1887 and 1893, over 11,000 farm mortgages were foreclosed in Kansas alone; mortgage companies owned three-fourths of all the land in fifteen counties in the state. Hoisting signs on their wagons, "In God We Trusted, in Kansas We Busted," many recent newcomers forlornly headed eastward from the disaster area. One observer wrote:

> There came through Emporia [Kansas] yesterday two old-fashioned wagons, headed east. . . . These movers were from western Kansas. . . . They had come from that wilderness only after a ten years' hard vicious fight, a fight which had left its scars on their faces, had beat their bodies, had taken the elasticity from their steps and left them crippled to enter the battle anew. For ten years they had been fighting the elements. They had seen it stop raining for months at a time. They had heard the fury of the winter wind as it came whining across the short burned grass and cut the flesh from their children huddling in the corner. These movers have strained their eyes watching through long summer days for the rain that never came. They had seen that big cloud roll up from the southwest about one in the afternoon, hover over the land, and stumble away with a few thumps of thunder as the sun went down. They have tossed through hot nights wild with worry, and have arisen only to find their worst nightmares grazing in reality on the brown stubble in front of their sun-warped doors. They had such high hopes when they went out there; they are so desolate now—no, not now, for now they are in the land of corn and honey. They have come out of the wilderness, back to the land of promise.[11]

[11] Quoted in Morison and Commager, *Growth*, 2: 238.

Drought and disaster in the 1880's and 1890's set the stage for serious agrarian political action. Groups known as Farmers' Alliances were organized in local chapters throughout the Midwest and South during the 1880's. The Alliance movement succeeded the Greenback party as the farmers' chief political vehicle.

The elections of 1890 resulted in several victories for Alliance candidates. Important gains for the organization occurred in state governments throughout the Midwest; in Nebraska, men elected with Alliance support took control of both houses of the state legislature, and in Kansas they won a majority in the lower house. The states of Kansas, Nebraska, and Minnesota sent eight Alliance-supported Congressmen to Washington, and William A. Peffer of Kansas and James H. Kyle of South Dakota—both endorsed by the Alliance—were elected to the United States Senate. These men all promoted railroad regulation, debt easement, and other measures that farmers demanded.

In the South, candidates with Alliance support were equally successful. "Pitchfork Ben" Tillman organized small farmers and got himself elected governor of South Carolina, while John L. M. Irby was elected to the Senate from that state. In Georgia, six congressmen supporting the farmers' demands won elections, including Thomas E. Watson. The farmers also won victories in Alabama, North Carolina, Florida, Virginia, Missouri, and Texas.

In 1891, under the leadership of Ignatius Donnelly and James B. Weaver, Alliance representatives from the South and Midwest met at Cincinnati to begin uniting farmers on a national level. They convened again in St. Louis in February, 1892, and laid the groundwork for a national third party. Members of the St. Louis convention called for a meeting on July 4 in Omaha to nominate candidates for president and vice-president. There James B. Weaver got the presidential nod.

The People's or Populist party, as it was called, drew support from others besides farmers. Included in its ranks were former Greenbackers, members of the Knights of Labor, people from all walks of life who favored inflation, and followers of Edward Bellamy and Henry George. Many observers considered its platform highly radical, even dangerous. The money question had evolved to the issue of free coinage of silver—the notion that the government should mint an unlimited number of silver dollars from the West's ample silver reserves, thus increasing the amount of money in circulation. The platform also demanded government control of all currency—at that time certain national banks could issue paper money of their own—and called for government ownership of railroads and telephone and telegraph systems. The Populists also proposed several political reforms, including the secret ballot, the election of U.S. senators by popular vote rather than by state legislatures, the referendum, and the initiative—this last a process by which voters could directly introduce bills into state legislatures. The party bid for widespread labor support by advocating the eight-hour day and condemning the federal government's unrestricted immigration policy. The introduction to the platform, drawn up by Ignatius Donnelly, painted a grim picture of America:

> We meet in the midst of a nation brought to the verge of moral, political, and material ruin. Corruption dominates the ballot-box, the legislatures, the Congress, and touches even the ermine of the bench. The people are demoralized. . . . The newspapers are largely subsidized or muzzled; public opinion silenced; business prostrated; our homes covered with mortgages; labor impoverished; and the land concentrating in the hands of the capitalists. The urban workmen are denied the right of organization for self-protection; imported pauperized labor beats down their wages; a hireling standing army, unrecognized by our laws, is established to shoot them down, and they are rapidly degenerating into European conditions. The fruits of the toil of millions are boldly stolen to build up colossal fortunes for a few, unprecedented in the history of mankind; and the possessors of these, in turn, despise the republic and endanger liberty. From the same prolific womb of governmental injustice we breed the two great classes—tramps and millionaires.[12]

[12] Quoted in ibid., pp. 240–241.

Prominent among Populist campaign speakers were Mary Ellen ("Mary Yellin'") Lease, who urged farmers to raise less corn and more hell as she raged against the "bloodhounds of money" on Wall Street, and "Sockless Jerry" Simpson, probably the only man ever to achieve immortality by being accused of going without stockings. Rural people came from miles around on horseback, in buggies, and on springless flat-bed farm wagons to hear and applaud the Populist gospel. As one writer noted,

> The upheaval that took place . . . was a religious revival, a crusade . . . in which a tongue of flame sat upon every man and each spake as the spirit gave him utterance. . . .
>
> The farmers, the country merchants, the cattle-herders, they of the long chin-whiskers, and . . . the broad-brimmed hats . . . had also heard the word and could preach the gospel of Populism. . . . Women with skins tanned to parchment by the hot winds, with bony hands of toil . . . could talk in meeting, and . . . right straight to the point.[13]

Kansas State Historical Society, Topeka

"Sockless Jerry" Simpson, photographed during a political debate at Harper, Kansas, in 1892.

James B. Weaver made a good showing in 1892, better than most third-party presidential candidates. He might have done even better had his campaigning in the South not been curtailed after he received unfavorable publicity concerning his career as a Union general during the Civil War. As it was, Weaver polled a million votes out of a total of approximately twelve million votes cast; he carried the states of Idaho, Colorado, Kansas, and Nevada, while North Dakota and Oregon gave him one electoral vote each. Support for Populist candidates in the South was slight, owing largely to Democratic ballot-box stuffing and the doctrine of white supremacy.

Thomas E. Watson and Southern Populism

During the 1892 campaign, Populists led by Georgia's Thomas E. Watson had tried to form a coalition of white and Negro farmers in the South. The interests of the two groups, after all, were similar. Black as well as white

[13] Quoted in John D. Hicks, *The Populist Revolt: A History of the Farmers' Alliance and the People's Party* (Lincoln: University of Nebraska Press, 1931), p. 159.

Thomas E. Watson.

Culver Pictures

Farmers' Alliance chapters had been formed, and they often met jointly and cooperated for political purposes. But Watson's attempt foundered on the rock of white supremacy. After the withdrawal of federal troops from the South in 1877, whites had moved back into control and had begun to pass the Jim Crow laws that would eventually seal off blacks from social, political, and economic advantage. The southern ruling class, composed of sometimes impoverished members of the planter aristocracy and the rich new capitalists of the postwar period, feared any white-black alliance that might threaten them politically or economically. Many southern politicians stuck with the Democrats and demogogically whipped up fears of black domination, tarring the Populists with the label "nigger party."

Despite opposition, Tom Watson of Georgia persisted in his efforts to bring the two races together in a common cause. "Now consider," he said,

> here were two distinct races dwelling together, with political equality established between them by law. They lived in the same section; won their livelihood by the same pursuits; cultivated adjoining fields on the same terms; enjoyed together the bounties of a generous climate; suffered together the rigors of cruelly unjust laws; spoke the same language; bought and sold in the same markets; classified themselves into churches under the same denominational teachings; neither race antagonizing the other in any branch of industry; each absolutely dependent on the other in all the avenues of labor and employment; and yet, instead of being allies, as every dictate of reason and prudence and self-interest and justice said they should be, they were kept apart, in dangerous hostility, that the sordid aims of partisan politics might be served.[14]

Watson firmly believed that the Populist movement would do much to cement race relations and place some power in the hands of dispossessed rural southerners:

[14] Thomas E. Watson, "The Negro Question in the South," *The Arena* 6 (October 1892): 542.

> The People's party will settle the race question. First, by enacting the Australian [secret] ballot system. Second, by offering to white and black a rallying point which is free from the odium of former discords and strifes. Third, by presenting a platform immensely beneficial to both races and injurious to neither. Fourth, by making it to the *interest* of both races to act together for the success of the platform. Fifth, by making it to the *interest* of the colored man to have the same patriotic zeal for the welfare of the South that the whites possess.[15]

Negroes in 1892 supported Watson's appeal with considerable enthusiasm. Watson appeared on platforms with black Populists and called on white listeners to defend blacks' constitutional rights. In many areas, Negroes supported Populism despite intimidation and violence more severe than they had encountered during Reconstruction. One of Watson's most effective workers was H. S. Doyle, a black preacher who made several speeches urging Watson's re-election to Congress in 1892. Threatened with lynching, Doyle fled to Watson for protection, and Watson's call for aid was answered by two thousand armed white farmers.

But all the effort was to no avail. Demagoguery won in the end, and the races were not brought together. W. E. B. Du Bois, a famous Negro leader and writer not given to uncritical praise for southern white politicians, regarded Watson's failure as a calamity for the black race. Had the coalition Watson attempted to mold succeeded, Du Bois wrote, the history of the South and that of black America might have been much different.

Watson himself eventually abandoned the cause and turned his back on southern Negroes. Quoting him in part, C. Vann Woodward has written:

> "The white people dare not revolt so long as they can be intimidated by the fear of the negro vote," he explained. Once the "bugaboo of negro domination" was removed, however, "every white man would act according to his own conscience and judgment in deciding how he shall vote."

[15] Ibid., p. 546.

> With these words Watson abandoned his old dream of uniting both races against the enemy, and took his first step toward the opposite extreme in racial views. There was another consideration which he did not mention. With the Negro vote eliminated, Watson and the Populists stood in much the same relation toward the two factions of the Democratic party as the Negro had occupied toward Populists and Democrats: they held the balance of power.[16]

This grip on the balance of power proved to be of little value. The Populist party began to decline in influence after 1892, in the South and elsewhere. Despite the gains in the West, where Populists had elected governors in Colorado, Kansas, North Dakota, and Wyoming, the party's rank-and-file membership was captured by the Democrats in 1896. By then the most popular and important demand was the free coinage of silver, and the Democratic party simply incorporated it.

William Jennings Bryan and Free Silver

In 1896 the issue was once again cheap money and inflation. Millions of farmers and workingmen, many of them former members of the Greenback party, had responded to the Populists' proposal for the free coinage of silver, and they were supported by the owners of western silver mines. Basically, the free silverites demanded that the government abandon the gold standard in favor of a bimetallic standard by producing silver dollars as well as gold dollars and paper currency backed by gold reserves. Regular Democrats under the leadership of Grover Cleveland, who was president from 1885 to 1889 and again from 1893 to 1897, stood solidly against bimetallism and for maintenance of the gold standard. They believed that the minting of an unlimited number of silver dollars would bring economic disaster. They pointed out, correctly, that money itself has no fixed value. A dollar represents a certain quantity of the goods and services available in the nation. If the total number of dollars were increased without increasing the

[16] C. Vann Woodward, *Tom Watson, Agrarian Rebel* (New York: Oxford University Press, 1963), pp. 371–372.

total quantity of goods and services available, the dollar would simply buy less, bringing inflation. But inflation was precisely what the farmers wanted—if the dollar dropped in value, their crops would bring in more money while their existing debts for loans and mortgages would remain the same. The fact that any future loans and mortgages would become more expensive—as would the manufactured goods they had to buy—was of secondary importance. Cleveland clearly was not in step with the changes taking place within the Democratic party. About Cleveland, historian Thomas A. Bailey wrote the following:

> As an ultra-conservative worshipper of the status quo, lawyer Grover Cleveland was a Hamiltonian Democrat and, like Hamilton, a "traitor" to the non-affluent class from which he had risen. Also, like Hamilton, he was more concerned with law, order, and property rights than with human rights.[17]

The issue split the ranks of the Democratic party. Northeastern Democrats tended to support Cleveland and the gold standard. To Democrats in other parts of the country, however, free silver began to sound like a good idea. Before the Democratic convention of 1896, a group of western Democrats issued the following statement:

> We believe that the establishment of gold as the only monetary standard and the elimination of silver as a full legal tender money, will increase the purchasing power of each dollar, add to the burden of all debts, decrease the market value of all other forms of property, continue and intensify business depression, and finally, reduce the majority of the people to financial bondage.[18]

These Democrats believed that their statement reflected the sentiments of the majority of the party and that it should become part of the party's campaign platform.

[17] Thomas A. Bailey, *Presidential Greatness* (New York: Appleton-Century, 1966), p. 301.

[18] Quoted in William Jennings Bryan, *The First Battle* (Chicago: W. B. Conkey Co., 1896), p. 156.

A young politician from Lincoln, Nebraska, William Jennings Bryan, was one of the statement's sponsors. Bryan had moved to Lincoln in 1887 after practicing law for three years in Jacksonville, Illinois. Not deeply interested in law, he entered politics in 1890, becoming the Democratic candidate for Congress in a Republican district and winning by a 6,713-vote majority. Re-elected in 1892, he was defeated two years later in a bid for the Senate. After that, Bryan became editor of the Omaha *World-Herald* and on the side developed a devoted following as a lecturer on Chautauqua tours—popular road shows which took entertainment and education into the small towns of the hinterland. Bryan had identified himself with the silver men in the Democratic party; he and his supporters were determined to gain control of the national convention in 1896, and they did.

The convention refused by a 564-to-357 vote to endorse its own Democratic administration, thus repudiating President Cleveland. This set the stage for Bryan. Known by then as "the Boy Orator of the Platte"—one of his critics remarked that the Platte River was "six inches deep and six miles wide at the mouth"—Bryan moved to the platform to deliver the speech that has become one of the most famous in American history. After thoroughly and at great length castigating trusts, banks, Republicans, and Gold Democrats—derisively called "Gold Bugs"—Bryan shifted into a really high rhetorical gear:

> It is the issue of 1776 all over again. Our ancestors, when but three millions in number, had the courage to declare their political independence of every other nation; shall we, their descendants, when we have grown to seventy millions, declare that we are less independent than our forefathers? No, my friends, that will never be the verdict of our people. Therefore, we care not upon what lines the battle is fought. If they say bimetallism is good, but that we cannot have it until other nations help us, we reply that, instead of having a gold standard because England has, we will restore bimetallism, and then let England have bimetallism because the United States has it. If they care to come out in the open

> field and defend the gold standard as a good thing, we will fight them to the uttermost. Having behind us the producing masses of this nation and the world, supported by the commercial interests, the laboring interests, and the toilers everywhere, we will answer their demands for a gold standard by saying to them: "You shall not press down upon the brow of labor this crown of thorns, you shall not crucify mankind upon a cross of Gold."[19]

The "Cross of Gold" speech swept the convention into pandemonium. Carried along by the tide of wild enthusiasm Bryan had generated, the delegates nominated the thirty-six-year-old silver-tongued orator on the fifth ballot. A demand that the government coin silver at a ratio to gold of sixteen to one became the party's major platform plank. Thoroughly defeated, Gold Democrats left the convention and, for the most part, sat out the campaign in silence.

The Republican Response

The Republican party took the opposite position on the silver issue. Its platform contained this statement concerning silver coinage:

> We are unalterably opposed to every measure calculated to debase our currency or impair the credit of our country. We are, therefore, opposed to the free coinage of silver except by international agreement with the leading commercial nations of the world, which we pledge ourselves to promote, and until such agreement can be obtained the existing gold standard must be preserved. All our silver and paper currency must be maintained at parity with gold, and we favor all measures designed to maintain inviolably the obligations of the United States and all our money, whether coin or paper, at the present standard, the standard of the most enlightened nations of the earth.[20]

[19] Ibid., p. 206.
[20] Quoted in ibid., p. 169.

Not all Republicans supported this position. Republican senators from the silver states—Henry M. Teller of Colorado, Fred T. Dubois of Idaho, R. F. Pettigrew of South Dakota, Frank Cannon of Utah, and Lee Mantle of Montana—opposed the party attitude on coinage, winning as a result the name "Silver Republicans." They refused to support William McKinley, the Republican presidential nominee.

As the campaign progressed, the coinage issue became more emotional than rational. Those who opposed the free coinage of silver forecast a complete collapse of the American financial structure should the sixteen-to-one ratio ever be enacted into law. The silver forces proclaimed "sixteen to one" as the cure for all the nation's ills, financial and otherwise. The following statement by Silver Republicans was typical:

> The restoration of bimetallism by this country will double the basis of our money system—in time it will double the stock of primary money of the world—will stop falling prices and steadily elevate them until they will regain their normal relation to the volume of debts and credits in the world. Bimetallism will help to bring about the great hope of every social reformer, every believer in the advancement of the race, who realize that the instability of prices has been the deadly foe of our toilers and the servant of the foreign interest gatherer. Bimetallism will help to bring the time when a certain expenditure of human toil will produce a certain financial result. Who among the great masses of our people in the United States but feels that his lot would be made better, his aspirations take new wings, if he could know in the performance of his labor what would be the price of his product?[21]

The free-silver issue transcended party loyalties, the Silver Republicans said; they urged all those who believed in free silver to vote for William Jennings Bryan.

[21] Quoted in ibid., p. 180.

The Populists in 1896

The Populists were left out in the cold, their principal issue, bimetallism, stolen by the Democrats. Nevertheless, they met in convention in St. Louis in July, 1896, to consider their next move. The immediate and overriding problem was whether or not they should nominate their own presidential candidate. Most southern delegates opposed support for Bryan because they were convinced that a Populist-Democratic fusion would kill Populism in the South. A diverse group of northern delegates opposed Bryan's endorsement with equal vigor; they believed that it would compromise the Populist party on almost every point except the money question and would lead to the destruction of the party. This group included Senator William A. Peffer of Kansas, Ignatius Donnelly of Minnesota, writer Henry Demarest Lloyd and lawyer Clarence Darrow of Chicago, labor leader Robert Schilling, and Jacob S. Coxey of Ohio, a wealthy quarry owner who had led a ragged band of unemployed men in a march on Washington in 1894. But Bryan supporters were in control of the convention. At the opening session, the chairman inquired:

> Do you want McKinley, and Government bonds and national bank issues, and high taxation, and a government by injunction? Do you want any or all of these, or would you rather have an enlarged volume of money and greater prosperity? Are you in favor of an income tax, or would you rather have the chief executive appoint a few more [justices] to the Supreme Court to declare the income tax unconstitutional, or do you want a President who is in favor of lightening the burdens of the people? A man that is in favor of Government ownership of railroads and telegraphs? If you were compelled to take your choice between men advocating these different principles of government, which would you take? I am not here advocating Mr. Bryan's nomination. Do not misunderstand me that I am advocating a specific choice for you to make. It is for you to choose and not for me. If by putting a third ticket in the field you would defeat free coinage; defeat a withdrawal of the [currency] issue power of national banks;

> defeat Government ownership of railroads, telephones and telegraphs; defeat an income tax and foist gold monometallism and high taxation upon the people for a generation to come, which would you do? It is for you to choose and not for me, but you should choose wisely, as doubtless you will.[22]

To most of the delegates, choosing Bryan seemed the better part of wisdom. Stating that the time had come for the free-silver forces to combine to defeat the "confederated gold powers," James B. Weaver offered Bryan's name in nomination. Weaver pointed out that Bryan's campaigns for Congress in Nebraska had always received Populist endorsement in that state, and he praised Bryan as the "matchless champion of the people, that intrepid foe of corporate greed." The convention went along with Weaver. Bryan was now both the Democratic and the Populist nominee for president.

Many Populist leaders were extremely disappointed. Henry Demarest Lloyd wrote that the convention was the most discouraging experience of his life. He considered the free-silver movement a trap. Free silver should have been only one issue among many; it was not important enough to justify betrayal of the rest of the party's platform. He summed up the convention this way:

> The National Convention was gagged, clique-ridden, and machine ruled. Members who were opposed to the plans they knew to be afoot to deliver the People's party to the Democracy [Democratic party] were privately informed with cynical frankness by the presiding officer that he would never allow them to catch his eye to get the floor. The Committee on Resolutions was packed and summarily squelched any attempt to get into the platform anything that would endanger the leader's plans of fusion. When the platform was reported to the Convention, the previous question was at once moved and declared carried, and

[22] Quoted in ibid., pp. 269–270.

> the party went into the campaign on a declaration of principles, of which the delegates who adopted it knew only so much as they had been able to catch, as it was read rapidly, amid the tumult and disorder of a convention of fifteen hundred, surrounded by a noisy audience of thousands of onlookers.[23]

Campaign and Election, 1896

William Jennings Bryan's campaign in 1896 revolutionized American politics. He traveled thousands of miles—a departure from customary campaign technique—and made more than five hundred speeches, a total of thirty-six on one particular day. William McKinley, on the other hand, ran a "front-porch campaign," receiving delegations of supporters and well-wishers at his home in Canton, Ohio, while industrialist Mark Hanna organized and managed the troop of speakers who represented McKinley and Republican conservatism throughout the country. Republican leaders were sufficiently worried about Bryan to pour millions of dollars into the campaign. Industrialists and businessmen contributed heavily to the Republican war chest, and the Grand Old Party far outspent the Democrats, disbursing $16 million to their opponents' $1 million, coincidentally reflecting the ratio at which Democrats wished to coin silver. Republican speakers made "Stop Bryan, Save America" their theme and concentrated mainly on "belly issues," making much of the slogan "McKinley and the Full Dinner Pail." Meanwhile, the country was pulling out of the deep depression that had begun in 1893 and the price of wheat was going up. This did not harm the Republican cause.

State Historical Society of Colorado

William Jennings Bryan was sometimes called "the Commoner," a name he gave to the newspaper he published after 1900.

Concentrating on free silver, monopolies, and trusts, Bryan represented a revolt against industrialization; his followers were, in the main, Americans who objected to

[23] Quoted in Caro (Caroline A.) Lloyd, *Henry Demarest Lloyd* (New York: G. P. Putnam's Sons, 1912), pp. 261–262.

the power held by the new industrial class. Said Bryan at one point to educate his rural listeners about monopolies:

> The essential thing in monopoly is the suspension of the law of competition. If an individual, or a group of individuals acting in concert control all of a certain product, or a sufficient amount to enable them to arbitrarily fix the price of the thing produced, they have what is called a monopoly. When such a monopoly is in private hands, the public has no protection from the selfish interest and greed of those at the head of the monopoly. It is because human beings cannot be entrusted with such power that the Democratic party has denounced a private monopoly as indefensible and intolerable.[24]

The silver issue, however, received the most attention. Wealthy conservatives blanched at the thought of free silver; the inflation it would bring would reduce the value of their holdings perhaps by half. "In God We Trust, with Bryan We Bust," Republican speakers warned. Many of Bryan's followers, on the other hand, envisioned the gates of heaven opening as the mints spewed out silver coins. As historian Thomas A. Bailey has remarked,

> Free silver became almost as much a religious as a financial issue. Hordes of fanatical free-silverites hailed Bryan as the Moses to lead them out of the wilderness of debt. Lusty-throated followers sang, "We'll All Have Our Pockets Lined with Silver" and "No Crown of Thorns, No Cross of Gold."[25]

This fervent, unrestrained religiosity, plus continual Populist jeering at solid Republicans, finally drove the editor of a small-town Kansas daily, the *Emporia Gazette*, to sit down and write a scathing editorial and gain a na-

[24] William Jennings Bryan, *The Commoner Condensed* (New York: Abbey Press, 1902), p. 364.

[25] Thomas A. Bailey, *The American Pageant: A History of the Republic* (Boston: D. C. Heath, 1956), p. 600.

tional reputation. "What's the matter with Kansas?" asked conservative William Allen White.

> We all know; yet here we are at it again. We have an old moss-back Jacksonian who snorts and howls because there is a bathtub in the State House; we are running that old jay for Governor. . . . We have raked the old ash heap of failure in the state and found an old human hoop skirt who has failed as a businessman, who has failed as an editor, who has failed as a preacher, and we are going to run him for Congressman-at-Large. . . . Then for fear some hint that the state had become respectable might percolate through the civilized portions of the nation, we have decided to send three or four harpies out lecturing, telling the people that Kansas is raising hell and letting the corn go to weeds.
>
> Oh, this is a state to be proud of! We are a people who can hold up our heads! . . . We don't need population, we don't need wealth, we don't need well-dressed men on the streets, we don't need cities in the fertile prairies; you bet we don't. What we are after is the money power. Because we have become poorer and ornerier and meaner than a spavined, distempered mule, we, the people of Kansas, propose to kick; we don't care to build up, we wish to tear down. . . .
>
> Give the prosperous man the dickens! . . . Put the lazy, greasy fizzle who can't pay his debts on the altar and bow down and worship him. Let the state ideal be high. What we need is not the respect of our fellowmen, but the chance to get something for nothing.[26]

A week later, historian Eric Goldman has written, White returned from a trip to Denver to find himself a celebrity.

> "What's the Matter with Kansas?" was being quoted, reprinted, praised throughout urban America; letters were streaming in from bankers and workingmen, from housewives and the Speaker of the United States House of

[26] Quoted in Eric Goldman, *Rendezvous with Destiny: A History of Modern American Reform* (New York: Random House, Vintage Books, 1956), pp. 52–53.

> Representatives. Just as Henry George, two decades earlier, vaulted to fame by voicing the anger from the bottom, now another writer was winning widespread repute as the spokesman of the middle-class mood. The nice young man in the linen suit had spoken for all those who wanted their politics starched with respectability. The town editor who saw Populist doctrine as the enemy of prosperity had reacted for millions in the urban areas, for clerks and factory hands no less than for professors and manufacturers.[27]

Despite the Republicans' use of fear psychology, their huge campaign expenditures, and signs that the depression was ending, Bryan received a respectable popular vote. Returns gave him 6.4 million to McKinley's 7 million, and 176 out of 447 electoral votes. Business, industry, and conservatism had been shaken, although they were far from defeated. More than anything else, perhaps, the campaign altered the course of the Democratic party. It emerged as the party opposed to trusts, high tariffs, injunctions as strikebreaking weapons, and conservative court decisions limiting labor's right to organize and strike and denying the regulatory powers of the federal government.

Eric Goldman has analyzed the election of 1896 in this way:

> Bryan, the Democrat, swept the Democratic South and held much of the normal machine vote. Bryan, the most convenient outlet for protest against business America, carried most of the embittered agrarian states of the West. In all, the Democratic-Populist nominee came within 600,000 of equaling McKinley's record 7,000,000 votes. Yet this strong showing did not, by any means, indicate a genuinely national sentiment. At a time when every third American lived in a community of more than four thousand people, Bryan carried only overwhelmingly agricultural states. He lost every state in the industrializing east-central and middle-Atlantic areas and every county in the most industrialized section of the country, New England. Equally significant, crossing to the wrong side of the railroad tracks

[27] Ibid., p. 53.

> in towns or cities brought no relatively greater support for Bryan. The huge slush funds spent by the Republicans and the intimidation of industrial workers practiced by many employers had something to do with the result, but these were hardly the essential story. The essential story was that reform associated with shaggy agrarianism could not carry a swiftly industrializing, swiftly urbanizing nation.[28]

The Populist Party and Its Influence

The Democratic theft of Populist issues all but finished the Populist party as a political power. In 1900 the Populists again supported William Jennings Bryan, who was again the Democratic nominee for president. In that election, Bryan received a few less popular votes and twenty-two fewer electoral votes than he had four years before. In 1904 the Democrats went conservative and nominated Alton B. Parker, a highly respected but colorless New York lawyer. Thomas E. Watson then tried to revive the Populist party by running for president himself. Watson had never been a Bryan supporter; he distrusted the Democrats almost as much as he disliked the Republicans. "In the eight years in which Mr. Bryan has been at the front," Watson said,

> I had taken no hand in politics for I had no confidence in the promises of the Democratic leaders, and there was no chance to do business for the Populists while Mr. Bryan was claiming to be as good a one as could be desired. When Bryan left our platform I went upon it, determined that the country should at least be reminded that both the old parties were now equally Hamiltonian [business-oriented].[29]

Watson's campaign was a complete failure; he repeated it in 1908 with the same results. As a political force, the Populist party was dead. Populist ideas, however, were not.

William Jennings Bryan credited the Populist party with

[28] Ibid., pp. 53–54.

[29] Thomas E. Watson, "Why I Am Still a Populist," *The American Review of Reviews* 38 (September 1908): 304.

advancing such causes as tariff reform, the direct election of U.S. senators, the income tax, the initiative and the referendum, and municipal ownership of public utilities—all of which had been enacted into law by 1914. Bryan also acknowledged the Populists' influence on the Democratic party:

> No one who understands the history of the last ten years can doubt the influence which the Populist party has exerted upon public affairs. It has been a great educational factor and the Democratic party has strengthened rather than weakened itself by endorsing a number of propositions which are called "populistic." To repudiate our populist allies and surrender to the corporate influences which now dominate the Republican party would be as impolitic as it would be unpatriotic. The Democratic party has no reason for existence except to champion the cause of the people.[30]

In 1931, historian John D. Hicks published *The Populist Revolt,* in which he praised Populism as a positive and constructive force for freedom and democracy. Hicks maintained that the Populists anticipated and diagnosed some of the important political and economic problems of their time. They were, Hicks said, committed to serving the public interest and were not simply the class-conscious fanatics they were so often portrayed as being by their contemporaries.

On the other hand, historian Richard Hofstadter, a deep student of reformist movements, has concluded that the major Populist weakness lay in the fact that the party continually looked backward, trying to resurrect a past of rural simplicity, a task impossible to perform.

In his history of American reform, *Rendezvous with Destiny*, Eric Goldman acknowledges Populism's contributions to the reform legislation enacted during the progressive period, 1900 to 1914. But Goldman also pointed out that "progressivism was not simply the Populist buggy rolled out for a new century. More urban in its base, progressivism was much more genuinely concerned with the problems of labor, and was far more inclined to include

[30] Bryan, *Commoner Condensed*, p. 86.

small businessmen and white-collar workers in the groups it wanted to help. . . ."[31] Progressivism, Goldman went on to say, virtually gave up the Populist attempt to make the Southern Negro an equal citizen and it paid little attention to the Negro problem as a whole.

During the progressive period, the Federal Reserve Act was passed to regulate banking and the money supply, tariffs were reduced, and the products of child labor were excluded from interstate commerce. Some trusts were broken up and railroads and other businesses came in for greater regulation. Farmers benefited from the Federal Warehouse Act, which made it possible for them to store products at low rates, and the Farm Loan Act, which eased the rural mortgage burden. Both pieces of legislation were enacted in 1916. The country did not get free coinage of silver, but, partly as a result of Populist agitation, it did get numerous other laws reformers had long deemed necessary for the welfare of the nation and its people.

SUGGESTED READINGS

Buck, Solon J. *The Granger Movement: A Study of Agricultural Organization and Its Political, Economic and Social Manifestations, 1870–1880.* University of Nebraska Press, Bison Books.

Cunningham, Raymond J., ed. *The Populists in Historical Perspective.* D. C. Heath.

Destler, Chester M. *American Radicalism, 1865–1901.* Quadrangle Books.

Goldman, Eric F. *Rendezvous with Destiny: A History of Modern American Reform.* Random House, Vintage Books.

Hicks, John D. *The Populist Revolt: A History of the Farmers' Alliance and the People's Party.* University of Nebraska Press, Bison Books.

Pollack, Norman. *The Populist Response to Industrial America.* W. W. Norton.

Woodward, C. Vann. *The Strange Career of Jim Crow.* Oxford University Press, Galaxy Books.

[31] Goldman, *Rendezvous with Destiny,* p. 60.

Library of Congress

Young boys were employed in the mines to pick out worthless pieces of slate from the valuable coal. They worked from sunup to sundown, with few breaks to relieve the strain of their bent-over positions, and earned less than a dollar a day.

THE INDUSTRIAL WORKERS

Farmers in the nineteenth century had their troubles, but industrial workers in the cities, shackled to factory jobs and forced to exist in miserable slums and crowded tenements, lived continually perched on the edge of disaster. They depended entirely on wages for the necessities of life, and wages were low.

In 1880, the average industrial wage for men was $7.75 for a sixty-hour week. A decade later it had risen to $9.05, still hardly enough to support a family. As a consequence, to provide for the barest necessities,it was imperative that every member of a family above the age of nine or ten work. This was especially true in the textile industry, where in 1890 a total of 93,233 men, 43,213 women, and 2,839 children were employed in New England mills alone. Wages for women and children were substantially lower than those for men—averaging $5.53 a week for women and $2.65 a week for children. Six decades earlier, young girls fresh from the farm had earned $3.50 a week tending machinery in the mills. Working hours in 1890, as in 1830, were excessive, often as high as fourteen hours a day, six days a week. Most textile workers were unskilled, which placed them along with thousands of other laborers at the bottom of the industrial heap.

Working conditions in most factories—textile and others—were bad. Lighting was generally poor, ventilation usually nonexistent. Dangerous machinery more often than not went unguarded. Accidents—leaving workers maimed if not dead—were frequent. Coal mining was perhaps the most dangerous work of all. Explosions and cave-ins took hundreds of lives each year. Miners who escaped violent death had to contend with debilitating and sometimes fatal respiratory ailments brought on by the atmosphere of coal dust, noxious gases, and dampness in which they worked.

A young girl learning to operate a spinning machine in a textile factory, about 1909.

The Bettmann Archive, Inc.

Poor working conditions and low wages were inevitable results of the nineteenth-century concept of labor as a commodity. To most employers, wages and employee-related costs were simply expenses like any other expenses—for machinery or raw materials, for example—and the lower all such expenses could be kept, the greater the profits for the factory's owners. If an employee was dissatisfied with his wages or working conditions, he was free to sell his labor elsewhere. It was the individual worker's responsibility to look out for himself just as it was the factory owner's responsibility to look out for himself; each, by serving his own self-interest, would serve the best interests of the economy as a whole. Given this philosophy, it was not unnatural that employers would resist any pressures to increase wages or improve working conditions. They regarded unionization with particular disfavor. By organizing to improve their bargaining position, employers believed, workers were interfering with the free and healthy operation of the economy. By organizing, workers were also more likely to raise their employers' labor costs.

In 1886, labor leader George E. McNeill expressed the general attitude of workers of the time:

> We complain, that whereas labor produces all the wealth of the world, the laborer receives only as much as will keep him in the poorest condition of life to which he can be crowded down, for the shortest number of years; that he makes civilization possible, and is reduced to barbarism,—building houses not to own them, growing food he may not eat, and weaving raiment he may not wear; that all of the arts and comforts that lift human life above the brute are present to tantalize, and not to encourage him; that steam, electricity, chemistry and productive machinery are competitors, and not co-operators, with him; that the conditions of his employment are debasing, and not

> elevating,—demoralizing, and not self-controlling; and that, whereas he is the most important factor, he is treated as the least; that his home is in the tenement-houses, back-slums and alleys of the city, or the unhealthy lowlands of the suburbs; that his wife is forced from home, and his children from school; that he cannot, as a laborer, hope for thanks, honors or positions of trust; that he is practically debarred from representation or the public expression of his complaints. When at work, he belongs to the lower orders, and is continually under surveillance; when out of work, he is an outlaw, a tramp,—and he is a man without the rights of manhood,—the pariah of society, homeless, in the deep significance of the term.[1]

There was, for the laboring class, only one way to achieve a better deal—organize.

The National Labor Union

Labor organizations had long existed along craft lines, a tradition dating back to the guilds of the Middle Ages in Europe. Skilled craftsmen—shoemakers, pattern-makers, carpenters, and others—were, owing to their relative scarcity, considerably better off economically than the multitude of unskilled factory workers whose main jobs were tending machines. There was, however, little national cohesion among the craft unions; each organization tended to be local. And as industrialization progressed, machines more and more took the place of human labor, tending to decrease the need for skilled workers and increase the need for a large, unskilled and hence cheap work force. Factory-made furniture, for example, required the application of few of the skills of the cabinetmaker. Thanks to the flow of immigrants from Europe, there was always a surplus of unskilled labor, and as a result wages remained low.

The International Longshoremen's Association, founded in New York in 1892, included in its emblem the motto "All Work Is Noble."

Library of Congress

In seeking to form national unions, nineteenth-century labor leaders faced a two-pronged problem. They had to persuade members of diverse craft unions to cooperate without regard for craft lines, and they had to organize the

[1] George E. McNeill, ed., *The Labor Movement* (New York: A. M. Bridgeman, 1886), p. 455.

growing number of unskilled workers along new lines. Otherwise, labor generally would never be able to exert any real pressure on management to achieve higher wages, better working conditions, and other benefits. The two parts of the problem had to be solved simultaneously, labor leaders believed, if they were to have any hope for success. And, at least at first, they tended to think in terms of political rather than economic pressure—in terms of controlling blocs of votes in elections rather than bringing economic coercion to bear through strikes. For example, William H. Sylvis, president of the National Labor Union, spoke of the eight-hour day in the following context:

> While I am in favor of the eight hour system, I have always held it to be unwise and eminently foolish to attempt to enforce the system by strikes. What we want is agitation, education, and legislation. Convince the people that it is right, and then demand the necessary legislation. If our representatives refuse to give it to us, turn them out and put somebody in who will.[2]

But the futility of education and political action unreinforced by the use of economic power soon became pitifully clear to labor leaders.

William H. Sylvis.

Historical Pictures Service, Chicago

The National Labor Union, an organization its founders hoped would cut across craft lines and recruit both skilled and unskilled workers, was formed when delegates of several trade unions met in Baltimore in 1866. Sylvis became the union's first president. Greatly respected by the members, Sylvis had begun his career as an iron-molder in Pennsylvania, where he became a leader in an iron-molders' union and was largely responsible for the establishment of a national union of iron-molders in 1859.

Sylvis's approach to unionization was utopian. Strongly influenced by utopian cooperative movements that had achieved popularity before the Civil War, he believed that workers should establish their own businesses and industries, thus freeing themselves from capitalist control. Only

[2] Quoted in Terence V. Powderly, *Thirty Years of Labor* (Columbus, Ohio: Excelsior Publishing House, 1889), p. 474.

The New York Public Library

The execution of six Molly McGuires, members of a secret society of Irish miners who used violence to protest working conditions in the Pennsylvania coal fields.

in this way could workers end capitalist exploitation and the disregard for workers' welfare seemingly prompted solely by a greed for profits. Seeking wide labor support, Sylvis and other leaders of the National Labor Union urged the admission of women and blacks to membership. White male members were ready for neither, although the rank and file supported the idea of organizing all-black unions. Sylvis's utopianism was an anachronism in the America of the 1860's, and it attracted no political support. Three years after Sylvis died in 1869, the National Labor Union died too, although at its peak it had boasted 600,000 members.

The 1870's

The Panic of 1873 ushered in a depression and a long period of labor strife and turmoil. Unemployment rose rapidly and jobless men and women demonstrated for relief in New York, Chicago, Boston, Cincinnati, and Omaha. A committee representing New York's unemployed received permission to hold a meeting, which the mayor planned to address, in Tompkin's Square on January 13, 1874. At the last minute, city authorities cancelled the meeting. Unaware of this, a large crowd of men, women, and children gathered in the square hoping for word on the city's plans for relief for the poor and jobless. Some scuffling resulted, and mounted police moved in to disperse the crowd with clubs. Many people of all ages were badly injured.

In the anthracite coal fields of Pennsylvania, the terroristic Molly McGuires, a secret organization of Irish miners, were gathering momentum. Mine operators had cut wages contrary to agreements and had crushed strikes with armed force and strikebreakers. The Mollies struck back with sabotage, intimidation, murder, and beatings. Officials of the Philadelphia and Reading Railroad, which owned the mines, instigated some of the violence themselves, knowing that the Mollies would be blamed for it. They finally hired an agent of the Pinkerton detective agency, James McParlen, to infiltrate the organization. McParlen, using the alias McKenna, did his work well. Ten members of the Molly McGuires were indicted, tried, and convicted of murder and conspiracy. They were hanged. "No great strike was inaugurated by this secret organization," wrote one observer,

> but the murders, wreckings, and other actions by it caused a feverish condition of the public mind, so that when the great era of historic strikes really opened people feared for the continuance of industry and for the general prosperity and business of the country, and when the first great historic strike occurred in 1877 it is not to be wondered at that the public excitement was so great that the most drastic remedies were considered as the only ones with which to deal with labor uprisings and insurrections.[3]

Railroad Strikes

The convicted Mollies were hanged in 1876, the year before the outbreak of the most violent labor strife in American history up to that time. In July, 1877, Baltimore and Ohio Railroad workers called a strike to protest wage cuts.

[3] Carroll D. Wright, *The Battles of Labor* (Philadelphia: George W. Jacobs, 1906), pp. 112–113.

This action touched off a nationwide rail strike and much violence. The first incident occurred at Martinsburg, West Virginia, when strikers seized trains and other railroad property. The state militia was unable to restore order and federal troops were sent to the city. In Baltimore, widespread rioting brought in the militia; nine strikers were shot and killed before federal troops arrived. In Pittsburgh property damage reached $10 million and several deaths resulted from clashes between strikers and militia. Irving Werstein has described the railroad strife of 1877 in this way:

> Since they could not wholly depend on militia units, the railroad owners asked for Federal troops which President Rutherford B. Hayes promptly supplied. This inflamed the outraged public even further. Americans had been suffering from the worst depression in living memory. Hunger was everywhere and the poverty-stricken masses were infuriated at the sight of U.S. Regulars marching through the streets of their cities to defend millionaire railroad owners. In Baltimore, Pittsburgh, Chicago, St. Louis and San Francisco, thousands turned out to demonstrate against the soldiers.
>
> "We Want Bread Not Bayonets!" the mobs cried.
>
> But they received bullets and bayonets, not bread. The Regulars callously fired on the crowds. In Baltimore, an officer told his men, "The order is to shoot to kill! Those people are mutinous rabble, scurvy anarchists who deserve a bullet! I want them shot without mercy!"
>
> His men obeyed to the letter.
>
> Ten strikers were killed by army bullets. That blood-drenched July, over 100 persons were shot dead and more than 300 wounded by U.S. troops. This stern repression broke the strike, but its memory lingered on.[4]

The Knights of Labor

The Noble Order of the Knights of Labor had seized the faltering banner of industrial unionism from the National Labor Union in 1869 and went on to organize about 700,-

Irving Werstein, *The Great Struggle: Labor in America* (New York: Charles Scribner's Sons, 1965), p. 98. Copyright © 1965 Irving Werstein. Reprinted by permission of Charles Scribner's Sons.

000 workers by the mid-1880's. Founded by Uriah S. Stephens, the Knights of Labor became a secret organization with an elaborate ritual along the lines of the Masonic Order. According to its credo,

> Labor is noble and holy. To defend it from degradation; to divest it of the evils to body, mind, and estate which ignorance and greed have imposed; to rescue the toiler from the grasp of the selfish—is a work worthy of the noblest and best of our race. In all the multifarious branches of trade, capital has its combinations; and, whether intended or not, they crush the manly hopes of labor, and trample poor humanity in the dust. We mean no conflict with legitimate enterprise, no antagonism to necessary capital; but men, in their haste and greed, blinded by self-interests, overlook the interests of others, and sometimes violate the rights of those they deem helpless. We mean to uphold the dignity of labor, to affirm the nobility of all who earn their bread by the sweat of their brows. We mean to create a healthy public opinion on the subject of labor (the only creator of values), and the justice of its receiving a full, just share of the values or capital it has created. We shall, with all our strength, support laws made to harmonize the interests of labor and capital, and also those laws which tend to lighten the exhaustiveness of toil. . . .[5]

Terence V. Powderly became Grand Master Workman or president of the Knights of Labor in 1879. During the next several years the Knights won a few strikes for the eight-hour day, but lost a significant struggle against Jay Gould's railroad system, a struggle that Powderly had not supported. On May Day, 1886, the Knights staged demonstrations for the eight-hour day in many cities. But before the month of May was out, the union had received its death blow—the Chicago Haymarket riot.

Terence V. Powderly.

Brown Brothers

Haymarket

The background to the trouble in Chicago lay at the McCormick Harvester plant. According to Irving Werstein,

[5] Quoted in Carroll D. Wright, *The Industrial Evolution of the United States* (New York: Flood & Vincent, 1895), p. 247.

The management of the McCormick Harvester Works, which employed hundreds of mechanics, had taken a drastic step to throttle the eight-hour-day talk in the plant. Early in February, 1,000 union men had been locked out and replaced by scabs. Several hundred Pinkerton detectives and strong-arm goons were hired to "protect" the plant and company property. The union workers turned the lockout into a strike. They joined the May 1 movement and celebrated when the massive demonstration brought an eight-hour day to over 200,000 men and women in various parts of the country.

On May 3, two days after labor's greatest single offensive, a mass rally was held outside the McCormick Harvester Works. August Spies, a Chicago anarchist and labor leader, was among those who addressed the meeting. As his speech was reaching an impassioned climax in which he called upon the McCormick workers to hold firm, promising that their solidarity would soon bring them victory, the plant's gates swung open. Out charged scabs, Pinkertons and goons to attack the throng. In moments, bricks, rocks and fists were flying. A platoon of Chicago police dashed up with drawn revolvers. Someone yelled "Open fire!" A fusillade crackled. When the gunsmoke cleared, six union men were dead and twenty wounded.

This bloodthirsty violence aroused hot anger in Chicago's working-class districts. August Spies wrote an inflammatory leaflet which was headed Workers! To Arms! Take Revenge![6]

The next evening several thousand people appeared at Haymarket Square on Chicago's near west side to protest the killings. After several speeches rain began to fall and the meeting was breaking up when two hundred police arrived. Werstein continued:

The rain quickly reduced the audience to only 500 persons. At 10:15 P.M., Fielden, the evening's last speaker, was on the stand, making his concluding remarks. All at once, Captain Bonfield, whose men were drawn up behind

[6] Werstein, *The Great Struggle*, pp. 108–109.

him, loudly shouted, "I order you to disperse peacefully or take the consequences!"

Fielden stopped and smiled down from the platform. "Why, Captain, we are peaceable," he said. "Surely—"

He never finished the sentence.

A roar and a flash shattered the night. There were screams and shouts. Someone had thrown a bomb. The blast, which killed a police sergeant, was followed by shots as the officers fired point-blank into the crowd. Armed workers returned the fire. (It was not unusual for ordinary citizens to carry pistols in the Chicago of 1886.) When the shooting ended, seven policemen and four demonstrators were dead and possibly 200 people were wounded that night. The exact number of casualties could never be determined, nor was the person who threw the bomb ever found.[7]

Newspapers blamed the bomb-throwing on several anarchist leaders in Chicago and the public took its cues from the papers. Eight men were indicted and tried for conspiracy to commit murder. Judge Joseph E. Gary, who presided over the trial, stated that what they had

> shouted in speeches is enough for their condemnation and for the condemnation of all their co-conspirators. . . . They incited, advised, encouraged the throwing of the bomb that killed the policemen, not by addressing the bomb-thrower specially, and telling him to throw a bomb . . . but by general addresses to readers and hearers . . . instructing how to perform acts *within which* the act of throwing the bomb was embraced.[8]

Seven men were convicted of conspiracy and another was convicted as an accessory. The seven were sentenced to death, but on appeal for clemency two were given life imprisonment instead. One of the condemned committed suicide but the remaining four continued to proclaim their innocence, demanding freedom not clemency. Before their

[7] Ibid., p. 110.

[8] Joseph E. Gary, "The Chicago Anarchists of 1886," *The Century Magazine* 45 (April 1893): 812.

executions, two of them wrote to the governor of Illinois explaining why they would not sign a petition asking for leniency. One of them, Albert R. Parsons wrote:

> I am aware that petitions are being signed by hundreds of thousands of persons addressed to you, beseeching you to interpose your prerogative and commute the sentences of myself and comrades from death to imprisonment in the penitentiary. You are, I am told, a good constitutional lawyer and a sincere man. I, therefore, beg of you to examine the record of the trial, and then to conscientiously decide for yourself as to my guilt or innocence. . . . The records of the trial made in Judge Gary's court prove my innocence of the crime of murder. But there exists a conspiracy to judicially murder myself and imprisoned companions in the name of and by virtue of the authority of the state. . . . I am innocent, and I say to you that under no circumstances will I accept a commutation to imprisonment. In the name of the American people I demand my right, my lawful, constitutional, natural, inalienable right to liberty.[9]

Adolph Fischer, also condemned, told the governor:

> As a man of honor, as a man of conscience, and as a man of principle, I cannot accept mercy. I am not guilty of the charge in the indictment—of murder. I am no murderer, and cannot apologize for an action of which I know I am innocent. And should I ask "mercy" on account of my principles, which I honestly believe to be true and noble? No! I am no hypocrite and have, therefore, no excuses to offer with regard to being an Anarchist, because the experiences of the last eighteen months have only strengthened my convictions. The question is, Am I responsible for the death of the policemen at the Haymarket? and I say no, unless you assert that every Abolitionist could have been held responsible for the deeds of John Brown. Therefore, I could not ask, or accept "mercy" without lowering myself in my self-estimation. If I cannot obtain justice from the

[9] Quoted in Joseph R. Buchanan, *The Story of a Labor Agitator* (New York: The Outlook Co., 1903), pp. 383–384.

authorities, and be restored to my family, then I prefer that the verdict should be carried out as it stands.[10]

Six years after the four were hanged a new governor of Illinois, John Peter Altgeld, called the trial unfair and pardoned the three remaining prisoners. For this action Altgeld was publicly abused by conservatives—though praised by liberals—and defeated for re-election.

The Haymarket affair had done much harm to the American labor movement. In 1903, one organizer, socialist labor leader Joseph R. Buchanan, wrote:

> We looked upon the Haymarket affair as an impediment to our progress along educational lines, inasmuch as a majority of the people were unable to distinguish between anarchism and socialism.[11]

Buchanan was right, as a contemporary journalist noted:

> The common sense of the people has not taken the outbreak in Chicago as seriously as a mere newspaper reader might be led to believe, although it must be confessed that we Americans still sadly lack repose and self-possession, and are easily startled by sensational alarms. Thirty years ago a few men created a panic by shouting that the Pope was about to invade the country, and now the report of the Chicago bomb, through the cannon mouth of the press, has filled multitudes with dread lest the foundations of the social fabric should be on the point of giving way. It is as though, when we read that a cyclone has swallowed a village, we should begin to tremble lest the whole country be swept into the air. Our national inexperience, our rawness, our headlong, unreflecting energy, expose us to quick reactions. We are easily elated and easily depressed.[12]

The bombing at Haymarket Square helped bring down the Knights of Labor, an organization that had welcomed

[10] Quoted in ibid., pp. 384–385.

[11] Ibid., p. 298.

[12] J. L. Spaulding, "Are We in Danger of a Revolution?" *The Forum* 1 (July 1886): 409.

all American workers into its ranks without regard for type of employment, nationality, sex, creed, or color—60,000 blacks were members during the organization's peak in 1886. Although the Knights of Labor was not involved in the Haymarket affair, it was hurt by the general public backlash. This, combined with the failure of the Gould strike, various organizational weaknesses, and poor leadership on the part of Terence Powderly, was enough to do the Knights in. By 1890 the total membership was down to 100,000, and during that decade these few fused with other labor organizations.

Although the Knights of Labor enlisted Negroes, the organization was of another mind concerning Chinese. Thousands of Chinese had immigrated to the West Coast, many to find jobs as laborers in the 1860's on the Central Pacific Railroad then building east from California. By 1880 more than 75,000 Chinese lived in California, making up about nine percent of the state's population. They were not well treated. White workers, fearing for their jobs, persecuted Chinese laborers unmercifully. Bowing to California's demands, in 1880 Congress passed a law prohibiting Chinese immigration for ten years. Terence V. Powderly found no fault with white Americans persecuting Chinese, and he protested what he regarded as lax enforcement of the 1880 law:

> The great difficulty lay in detecting the difference between Chinamen, owing to the resemblance they bear to each other, gives rise to no end of trouble in preventing the coming of this servile race to America and the complaint of the people of the Western States and territories that the law is being constantly violated continues to be made.
>
> In desperation the people of the Pacific coast have petitioned and demanded of Congress to do something to enforce the law, but the Chinese still continue to come. In various places along the Pacific coast and in the territories the citizens of cities and towns have revolted against the presence of the Chinese, and in many instances violence has been resorted to. On September 2, 1885, the coal miners at Rock Springs, Wyoming Territory, massacred between

thirty and forty Chinese, burned their dwellings, and drove many others from the place. That this act of inhumanity and butchery is inexcusable is true, but the precedent had been established that the law could be violated with impunity by the Chinese, and those who desired to employ them. Exasperated at the success with which they had evaded the law, and insinuated themselves into their places along the Pacific railway, the white workmen became desperate and wreaked a terrible revenge upon the Chinese. Had steps been taken to observe the law, and had the Chinese been as rigidly excluded as they should have been, the workmen at Rock Springs would not have steeped their hands in the blood of a people whose very presence in this country is contamination, whose influence is wholly bad, and whose effect upon the morals of whatever community they inhabit tends to degrade and brutalize all with whom they come in contact.[13]

The New York Public Library

An anti-Chinese riot in Denver, Colorado, 1880.

[13] Powderly, *Thirty Years*, pp. 420–421.

The American Federation of Labor

As the Knights of Labor began to fade, a new union based on craft organization was emerging. This was the American Federation of Labor. The AFL from its beginning was interested only in bread-and-butter issues—shorter hours and higher pay for its members. The structure of the union differed from that of the Knights of Labor. "The Knights of Labor," wrote an observer in the 1890's,

> is an order composed of local and district assemblies of its own, and while the local assemblies may and do represent different trades and callings in life, they are nevertheless bound by one uniform system of laws and regulations, their ritual and proceedings being the same throughout the country; while the American Federation of Labor is a federation of various orders dissimilar in their methods of organization and having no common constitution or laws.[14]

Samuel Gompers became president of the AFL in 1886, the year the organization adopted its name. He presided not over a large centralized union, but over a group of independent craft unions, each self-governing, all loosely federated under the AFL. Under Gompers' leadership the AFL nearly doubled its membership—from 150,000 to almost 300,000—between 1886 and 1892.

Culver Pictures

Samuel Gompers.

Craft unions, then as later, discriminated against Negroes. Gompers began his career as a labor leader with a relatively enlightened attitude toward organizing Negro workers, but, as historian Bernard Mandel has commented,

> He sacrificed both his principles and the Negro workingman, as well as the broader interests of the whole labor movement, to the short-sighted and selfish demands of the aristocratic officialdom of the craft unions, whose spokesman he had agreed to be.[15]

Negroes by and large were excluded from craft unions and apprenticeship programs, a situation that has persisted in many instances to this day.

[14] Wright, *Industrial Evolution,* p. 250.

[15] Bernard Mandel, "Samuel Gompers and the Negro Workers, 1886–1914," *The Journal of Negro History* 40 (January 1955): 60. Copyright © 1955 by the Association for the Study of Negro Life and History.

Homestead

AFL membership passed a quarter of a million in 1892. The following year, depression once again visited the nation; industries cut wages and laid off workers by the thousands, bringing the most widespread labor unrest since the railroad strikes of 1877. In perhaps the most violent conflict, the Carnegie Steel Company pitted its corporate might against the Amalgamated Association of Iron, Steel and Tin Workers, a trade union belonging to the American Federation of Labor. In the summer of 1892, before the depression really hit, the union struck Carnegie, refusing to accept further reductions in wages. Considering working conditions in the mills, the men believed they deserved, if anything, wage increases, not reductions. And, as Leon Wolff has noted,

> aside from working conditions the accident rate was appalling. No over-all death and injury figures exist for 1892, but one may extrapolate backwards from certain statistics and contemporary writings to recreate the nightmare. In a single later year 195 men were killed in Pittsburgh's iron and steel mills; twenty-two from hot metal explosions, five from asphyxiation, ten from rolling accidents, seventy-three during the operation of cars and cranes, twenty-four from falling from heights or into pits, seven from electric shocks, eight while loading and piling, forty-six through miscellaneous causes. Total deaths in 1891 were probably around three hundred, because there was more handwork and less safety equipment. Accidents that year surely exceeded two thousand. Mechanization was still in its infancy and (especially in Bessemer processing) the men worked only inches away from brimming ladles of molten steel.[16]

Although the iron-workers' union admitted only skilled workers, its strike at the steel mills in Homestead, Pennsylvania, was supported by the entire work force there. At the time, Andrew Carnegie, the plant owner, was in Europe; Henry Clay Frick, the plant manager and a strong

[16] Leon Wolff, *Lockout* (New York: Harper & Row, 1965), p. 34.

anti-union man, was in charge. Frick closed the entire plant and refused to negotiate with the union. According to Irving Werstein:

> Frick was determined to break the union. . . . Even before the Amalgamated contract ran out, Frick ordered a high wooden fence crowned with barbed wire built around the plant. Rifle slits were cut in the wall and sentry boxes placed at its four corners. The workers dubbed the wall Fort Frick.
>
> On July 6, two days before the contract was to end, the manager announced a wage cut to be immediately effective. This brought vehement protests from the steel workers who held a demonstration climaxed by the burning of Frick in effigy. Frick used this "rowdiness" as an excuse to shut down the mill in a "protective measure" and locked out all workers, union and non-union alike. In this way Frick declared war against the Amalgamated Iron, Steel and Tin Workers.[17]

Library of Congress

The H. C. Frick Coke Company in the Connellsville region of Pennsylvania. This company had made Frick a wealthy man long before he became manager of Carnegie Steel in 1889.

On June 25, Frick had written Robert Pinkerton, head of the Pinkerton Detective Agency, the following letter:

> We will want 300 guards for service at our Homestead mills as a measure of precaution against interference with our plan to start operation of the works July 6th, 1892.
>
> The only trouble we anticipate is that an attempt will be made to prevent such of our men with whom we will by that time have made satisfactory arrangements from going to work, and possibly some demonstration of violence upon the part of those whose places have been filled, or most likely by an element which usually is attracted to such scenes for the purpose of stirring up trouble.
>
> We are not desirous that the men you send shall be armed unless the occasion properly calls for such a measure later on. . . .
>
> These guards should be assembled at Ashtabula, Ohio, not later than the morning of July 5th, when they may be taken by train to McKee's Rocks, or some other point upon the Ohio River below Pittsburgh, where they can

[17] Werstein, *The Great Struggle*, p. 123.

> be transferred to boats and landed within the enclosure of our premises at Homestead. We think absolute secrecy essential in the movement of the men. . . .
>
> As soon as your men are upon the premises we will notify the Sheriff and ask that they be deputized either at once or immediately upon an outbreak of such a character as to render such a step desirable.[18]

On July 6, two barges loaded with 300 Pinkerton detectives were towed up the Monongahela River. The strikers were ready. Foster Rhea Dulles has described the action:

> As the steel company's private army drew alongside the Homestead mills and prepared to land, there was a sudden exchange of shots between the barges and the shore. The workers had entrenched themselves behind a barricade of steel billets and as the Pinkertons tried to take possession of the plant, they were beaten back in a raging battle that swirled along the river front. All that day, from four in the morning until five in the afternoon, the fusillade of shots continued. The strikers set up a small brass cannon behind a breastwork of railroad ties and opened a direct fire on the barges. Failing to sink them, they poured barrels of oil into the river and set the oil afire. With three men already dead and many more wounded, the Pinkertons were trapped. Deserted by the tug which had towed them upstream, helplessly crowded into the barge which lay farthest from the shore, they finally ran up a white flag and agreed to surrender. In return for a guarantee of safe conduct out of the community, they gave up their arms and ammunition.
>
> But feelings were running too high at Homestead, where the casualties had included seven killed, for any easy re-establishment of order. When the Pinkertons came ashore, they were again attacked and had to run the gauntlet of an infuriated mob of men and women, armed with stones and clubs, before they were safely entrained for Pittsburgh. An uneasy calm then settled over the little town as the

[18] Quoted in Wolff, *Lockout*, p. 86.

Homestead workers, victorious in this first round, awaited the next moves by the company.[19]

Six days later the governor of Pennsylvania ordered 8,000 militiamen to Homestead, and, under the armed protection of the state, Frick reopened the plant with nonunion men. Strike leaders were charged with rioting and murder, and only 800 of the original 4,000 workers were rehired. One other event further aroused public sentiment against the strikers, which had been running high as it was:

> On July 23, a Russian-born anarchist, Alexander Berkman, who had no connection whatsoever with the strikers but had been aroused by the Carnegie Company's employment of Pinkerton operatives, forced his way into Frick's office in Pittsburgh and tried to assassinate him. Although shot and stabbed, the steel executive was not fatally injured and his assailant was captured. The assault had been planned by Berkman and his woman companion, Emma Goldman, a no less ardent advocate of "propaganda by deed," and only lack of funds to make the trip to Pittsburgh, as she later revealed in her autobiography, had prevented her from accompanying Berkman on his mission. He was sentenced to twenty-one years in prison for assault with intent to kill. Released after thirteen years of his term, he was later deported, together with Emma Goldman, to Soviet Russia.[20]

Library of Congress

Strikers watch the railroad station at Homestead, prepared to intercept any "scabs" imported by the company.

AFL leadership sat out the Homestead strike. Samuel Gompers offered the striking iron workers sympathy but nothing more. The iron workers went it alone and lost heavily. The steel industry was not to have another strong union until the 1930's. Although the Carnegie company prospered, the destruction of the union in 1892 brought abject poverty to steel workers generally. As Irving Werstein has said:

> The debacle at Homestead wrecked the union. The steel industry was not again to be effectively unionized for more

[19] Foster Rhea Dulles, *Labor in America: A History* (New York: Thomas Y. Crowell, 1968), p. 167. Copyright 1949, 1955, 1960 © 1966 by Foster Rhea Dulles. Reprinted with permission of the publisher, Thomas Y. Crowell Co., Inc.

[20] Ibid., p. 168.

> than forty years. During those weary decades steel workers lived on the edge of poverty. Skilled workers' wages fell almost 40 per cent; the rest slaved for only 16½ cents an hour. Homestead was a classic example of industrial ruthlessness as practiced by an American corporation in the 1890's.
>
> Frick abolished the 8-hour day in Homestead immediately following the strike. Two 12-hour shifts kept the plant going full blast all day, every day. The Carnegie Steel Company prospered as never before in its history. During the seventeen years prior to the strike it had amassed profits totalling $27,000,000. But in the nine years after the struggle, the company's profits soared to $106,000,000.
>
> The union's defeat had even more significance to the labor movement. It gave clear proof that the strongest craft union could not withstand the onslaught of a great corporation.[21]

Homestead was the biggest and bloodiest strike of the early 1890's. But there were others nearly as bloody—among metal miners in Coeur d'Alene, Idaho, railroad switchmen in Buffalo, New York, and coal miners in Tennessee. Many strikes in the 1890's were defeated by the use of state militia and federal troops, making government, in the eyes of labor, simply a tool of the capitalists. Samuel Gompers' lack of action during the Homestead strike lost him respect among a large segment of labor. Unskilled workers, receiving no attention from the AFL, had to look elsewhere for help.

The American Railway Union and the Pullman Strike

Certain railroad workers—such as engineers and brakemen—had long been organized into brotherhoods along craft lines. In June, 1893, the American Railway Union was formed to unite all skilled and unskilled workers—except Negroes—in the railroad industry. The decision to exclude blacks had been made despite strong pleas for their admission from the union's president, Eugene V. Debs. Debs did not resign his office, however, and under his leadership

[21] Werstein, *The Great Struggle*, p. 124.

the union conducted a successful strike against the Great Northern Railroad in April, 1894. George Pullman and his sleeping-car company were their next target for reform.

George Pullman.

Pullman-Standard

Paternalistic, feudal-minded George Pullman had established the town of Pullman, Illinois, in the 1880's as a benefit, he firmly believed, for his workers. Pullman, south of Chicago, was well designed with many modern facilities; it was called a "model town" by company officials, and in many respects it was. However, from the point of view of the workers, who were under strong company pressure to live in Pullman, the community had a few drawbacks.

> In the words of a company official, Pullman was a town "where all that is ugly and discordant and demoralizing is eliminated, and all that inspires to self-respect is generously provided." These were high-sounding words, but they fell flat on the ears of the workers who had to live there. The company owned the houses their employees lived in; it owned the stores, the library, the church, even the water and gas supply. The residents of Pullman had to buy at the company stores; they had to live in its houses and they paid whatever rates the company demanded.[22]

One Pullman worker put it a little more personally:

> We are born in a Pullman house, fed from the Pullman shop, taught in the Pullman school, catechized in the Pullman church, and when we die we shall be buried in the Pullman cemetery and go to the Pullman hell.[23]

The cost of living in Pullman, as Foster Rhea Dulles has pointed out, was far from low, nor was it in line with that of other communities:

> [Rents] for apartments in the model town, which in most instances had no bathtubs and one water faucet for every five families, were some twenty-five per cent higher than in nearby communities. A high premium was also charged for public utility services. "Oh, Hell!" the forthright Mark

[22] Ibid., p. 129.

[23] Quoted in Alice Gordon, *The Promise of America* (Chicago: Science Research Associates, 1970), p. 373.

> Hanna was quoted as commenting on his brother industrialist's baronial domain. "Model—. Go and live in Pullman and find out how much Pullman gets sellin' city water and gas ten per cent higher to those poor fools!"
>
> With the depression of 1893, the Pullman Company was for a time hard hit and after laying off more than 3,000 of its 5,800 employees, it cut the wages of those kept on from twenty-five to forty per cent without any corresponding reduction in rents for the company houses. The consequences were disastrous. A worker seldom earned as much as six dollars a week after the company had made its deductions [for food, rent, and other charges]. In one instance, an employee found that after payment for rent was taken out, his pay check came to two cents. "He never cashed it," the Reverend W. H. Carwardine, of the Pullman Methodist Episcopal Church reported. "He has it framed." And yet at the same time such things were happening, the Pullman Company kept on paying dividends [at the usual eight percent]. Even after business began to improve a little, enabling the company to take back some 2,000 of its employees, no steps were taken to restore the wage cuts or to reduce rents.[24]

Dulles drew material on which he based his statements from a federal government strike commission report of 1895. The report also noted:

> The company claims that it is simply legitimate business to use its position and resources to hire in the labor market as cheaply as possible and at the same time to keep rents up regardless of what wages are paid to its tenants or what similar tenements rent for elsewhere; to avail itself to the full extent of business depression and competition in reducing wages, and to disregard these same conditions as to rents. No valid reason is assigned for this position except simply that the company has the power and the legal right to do it.[25]

[24] Dulles, *Labor in America*, p. 172.

[25] Quoted in Leon Litwack, ed., *The American Labor Movement* (Englewood Cliffs, N. J.: Prentice-Hall, 1964), pp. 20–21.

Manufacturing sleeping cars was one part of the Pullman Company's business. Running a model town was another.

A committee representing workers who lived in the town finally met with George Pullman to plead for rent reductions. Pullman refused. Then, when three members of the committee were fired, workers—many of them members of the Railway Union—called a strike and shut down the entire plant.

Thanks in part to accounts of suffering by such journalists as Ray Stannard Baker, public sentiment favored the strikers. "Hardly less pitiful is the case of Andy Onda, a Greek, who lives with his wife and four little children in Room 8, tenement block H," ran one of Baker's stories:

> He made only $1.50 a day when the shops were running, and when the strike came on he was wholly out of money. He owes about sixty dollars for rent and supplies. Last Saturday he received his last supplies and yesterday afternoon his wife baked some hard biscuits on a neighbor's stove—having no fuel of her own—and when they were gone there was not enough left in the house to feed a mouse, to say nothing of four moaning children. Neither Onda's wife nor any of the children have any shoes to wear. Last week their water supply gave out, and being back on the rent the company would not repair the pipes, and Mrs. Onda has been compelled to carry water upstairs. Until recently she was accustomed to get fuel at the Pullman dump, but the company has placed its watchmen around that source of supply, and no striker's wife is allowed to approach. Every vestige of material suitable for burning has been picked up, and yesterday strikers with baskets were carrying away the refuse of the burned cars at Burnside.[26]

Lacking the power to oppose the company long on their own, union members among the Pullman strikers called for help from their president, Eugene V. Debs. Debs at first was reluctant to involve the entire union. According to Ray Stannard Baker,

[26] Ray Stannard Baker, *American Chronicle* (New York: Charles Scribner's Sons, 1945), p. 42. Copyright 1945 Ray Stannard Baker. Reprinted by permission of Charles Scribner's Sons.

> Compared with the vast issues that confronted him in his relationships with the western railroads it seemed a trifling issue. It ought to be settled by arbitration. But Debs was a sensitive and warm-hearted man. I remember thinking he resembled Bill Nye, the humorist, another midwesterner. He had the same gangling height, the same thinning hair and blue eyes. He was somewhat awkward, with an embarrassed gentleness of manner and a gift of explosive profanity. . . .
>
> I had liked him almost on sight, for I felt his unselfish devotion to the cause he was interested in. It was not primarily unionism, the organization, that absorbed him, as it did Gompers, but the human problems of the workingman. He was not so much concerned with the "aristocrats of labor," like the locomotive engineers, but with unorganized railroad workmen. He was for "clasping hands with the whole working class." When he refused a job that would have brought him several thousand dollars a year, in order to work for seventy-five dollars a month with the American Railway Union, he said,
>
> "I have a heart for others and that is why I am in this work. If I rise, it will be *with* the ranks, not *from* them."
>
> Though Debs had not wanted the Pullman strike, he was much moved and angered by the stories told by the striking workers. When he rose to speak at the convention [in 1894] he made a powerful and persuasive plea:
>
> "The time has come to strangle the Pullman monopoly. You will never be stronger for the conflict than you are now and you can go into it with a bright prospect of winning."
>
> His union gave Pullman five days to consider a settlement. Pullman's reply was: "We have nothing to arbitrate." He also said:
>
> "The workers have nothing to do with the amount of wages they shall receive; that is solely the business of the company."[27]

The American Railway Union joined the strike. Union members refused to work on trains carrying Pullman cars;

[27] Ibid., pp. 37–38.

Library of Congress

Federal troops guarding a mail train at Blue Island, Illinois, in 1894.

this tactic, in effect, broadened the strike to include numerous railroads.

Railroad companies naturally took Pullman's side in the dispute and formed the General Managers' Association to cooperate against the strikers. But when union men who cut Pullman cars from trains were fired, whole train crews walked off the job. By the end of July, every railroad in the Midwest was affected by the Railway Union's boycott. Debs counseled moderation and restraint and warned against the destruction of property. The situation remained peaceful until the managers imported strikebreakers and put into effect a plan to attach Pullman cars to mail trains. Interference with these trains would give management an excuse to call for federal help on the grounds that strikers were hampering the flow of United States mail. Strikers refused to distinguish between mail trains and any others that carried Pullmans.

At the request of railroad managers, United States Attorney General Richard Olney, himself a former railroad lawyer and completely without sympathy for labor, swore in 3,400 special deputies to run the trains. Violence resulted and railroad property was destroyed. Managers now appealed to President Grover Cleveland for troops, and got them.

> "The fat was in the fire once the soldiers came," wrote a *New York World* reporter. "Nothing in the world could then have prevented bloodshed. . . ."
>
> The strikers resented the army being used to protect the scabs who manned mail trains which were also used to haul freight and passengers. Resentment turned into hostility. Some strikers stoned a detail of soldiers and fighting broke out.
>
> Rifles cracked and bayonets flashed. Chicago was torn by near civil war as workers fought troops. During the course of the conflict army bullets and bayonets killed thirty strikers and wounded scores. But the strikers remained solid despite the "blue-bellies"—an 1894 slang term for U.S. soldiers.[28]

Public opinion now turned against the strikers, due in large part to unsympathetic stories in newspapers whose owners were strongly against the labor movement as a whole. "As disorder spread," wrote Foster Rhea Dulles,

> newspapers and magazines rang all the changes on the danger to society in what the *New York Tribune* declared to be "the greatest battle between labor and capital that has ever been inaugurated in the United States." It was almost universally insisted that "this rebellion must be put down" regardless of every other consideration. The attempt was made to draw a line between the railway workers and strike agitators. The former were said to be "the victims of selfish, cruel and insolent leaders" and all honest workingmen were called upon to free themselves from such "insufferable tyranny." The *New York Times* attacked Debs as "a lawbreaker at large, an enemy of the human race" and the *Chicago Herald* asserted that "short work should be made of this reckless, ranting, contumacious, impudent braggadocio. . . ."
>
> News stories carried alarming accounts of mob action

[28] Werstein, *The Great Struggle*, p. 132.

and battles with the police and troops. With such a newspaper as the *Washington Post* screaming in its headlines that "Chicago Is at the Mercy of the Incendiary's Torch," the general impression given was that the entire city was in the throes of revolution and anarchy. However a correspondent for the *New York Herald*, somehow keeping his balance amid such exaggerated fears and alarms, reported to his paper on July 9 that business was going on as usual, the stores were crowded with shoppers, and "there is no sign of mob or riot or strike, even, about the main part of the city."[29]

One public official protested President Cleveland's action —John Peter Altgeld, governor of Illinois. Altgeld wrote to the president:

> Surely the facts have not been correctly presented to you in this case or you would have taken the step; for it is entirely unnecessary and, as it seems to me, unjustifiable. Waiving all question of courtesy, I will say that the State of Illinois is not only able to take care of itself, but it stands ready today to furnish the Federal Government any assistance it may need elsewhere.[30]

Cleveland, relying on reports from his attorney general and convinced that Governor Altgeld was deliberately ignoring rioting and property destruction in Chicago, replied:

> Federal troops were sent to Chicago in strict accordance with the constitution and the laws of the United States, upon the demand of the Post-Office Department that obstruction of the mails should be removed, and upon the judicial officers of the United States [saying] that process of the Federal courts could not be executed through the ordinary means, and upon abundant proof that conspiracies existed against commerce between the states. To meet these conditions, which were clearly within the province of Federal authority, the presence of Federal troops in the city of Chicago was deemed not only proper but necessary;

[29] Dulles, *Labor in America*, p. 177.

[30] Grover Cleveland, "The Government in the Chicago Strike of 1894," *McClure's Magazine* 23 (July 1904): 238.

> and there has been no intention of thereby interfering with the plain duty of the local authorities to preserve the peace of the city.[31]

Cleveland's reference to the federal courts involved one of the most controversial aspects of the Pullman strike. At the behest of railroad attorneys, Judge Peter J. Grosscup of Chicago had issued an injunction forbidding the obstruction of mails and any interference with interstate commerce. Included in the injunction was a provision prohibiting the union from asking railroad employees not to work.

Eugene V. Debs now faced the combined force of the executive and judicial powers of the federal government. In desperation he appealed to other labor leaders to call a general strike in support of his men. Samuel Gompers of the AFL refused. Debs then tried one more conciliatory move, offering to call off the strike if the Pullman Company agreed to rehire strikers. This offer was refused out of hand. When the strike did not end, Judge Grosscup had Debs and several other union men arrested for violating his injunction. This halted the strike, and effectively destroyed the American Railway Union.

Strikebreaking by injunction, a favorite tactic of management at that time, had won another important victory. Speaking of judicial power and the influence of a single judge, Governor Altgeld said:

> He can legislate for himself, and having done so can then turn around and arrest and imprison as many people as he pleases; not for violating any law but on the mere pretext that they had disregarded his injunction, and, mark you, they are not tried by a jury according to the forms of law, but the same judge who issued the ukase and who claims that his dignity was offended, himself tries the case, and whether anything is proven or nothing is proven he can send men to prison at pleasure and there is no remedy.[32]

Four factors, according to Henry Pelling, led to the

[31] Ibid., p. 239.

[32] John Peter Altgeld, *Live Questions* (Chicago: George S. Bowen & Son, 1899), p. 459.

failure of the Pullman strike and the destruction of the American Railway Union. One was the fact that when

> railroad employees went on strike, it was not difficult for the managers to find replacements in the existing state of reduced employment. A second factor was the hostility of the railway brotherhoods to the new union, which they realized was designed to replace their own organizations. They therefore did nothing to discourage their members from taking jobs vacated by strikers. Third, the companies, realizing that Debs' union constituted the most dangerous challenge to their authority that tney had yet had to face, co-operated closely through the General Managers' Association. Fourth—and this was decisive—the federal government, in the person of [Attorney General] Richard Olney . . . stepped in swiftly to secure injunctions against the interruption of the movement of mail and interstate commerce; and to enforce these injunctions, he prevailed upon [President] Cleveland to send in federal troops.[33]

President Cleveland's actions, in fact, were most decisive in breaking the strike. Cleveland was a strong defender of the new industrial status quo and had no sympathy for radicals like Debs. During the strike the president was reported to have said, "If it takes the entire army and navy of the United States to deliver a post card in Chicago, that card will be delivered."[34]

Eugene V. Debs and American Socialism

The United States Supreme Court upheld the contempt-of-court charges against Debs, and he was jailed for six months. That experience, plus the tribulations of the Pullman strike itself and the destruction of his union, led him into new paths of thought. Debs spent a great deal of his time in prison reading and studying, and upon his release

[33] Henry Pelling, *American Labor* (Chicago: University of Chicago Press, 1965), pp. 94–95.

[34] Thomas A. Bailey, *Presidential Greatness* (New York: Appleton-Century, 1966), p. 180.

he declared himself a convert to socialism. He had become convinced that only through socialism could the worker receive justice. He advocated political action by a party independent of both the Republicans and the Democrats. Although Debs supported William Jennings Bryan in 1896, he made the following observation four years later:

Eugene V. Debs.

Courtesy Chicago Historical Society

> Needless it is for me to say to the thinking working man that he has no choice between these two capitalist parties, that they are both pledged to the same system and that whether the one or the other succeeds, he will still remain the wage-working slave he is today.
>
> What but meaningless phrases are "imperialism," "expansion," "free silver," "gold standard," etc., to the wage-worker? The large capitalists represented by Mr. McKinley and the small capitalists represented by Mr. Bryan are interested in these "issues," but they do not concern the working class.[35]

What did concern the workers, according to Debs, was the abolition of private ownership of the means of production and distribution.

Debs helped form the Socialist Democratic party in 1897, and in 1900 he ran for president on that party's ticket, receiving 96,116 votes. All told, Debs was to run for president five times as a socialist. He received 402,321 votes in 1904; 420,973 votes in 1908; and 901,062 votes in 1912. He declined the nomination in 1916, but America's entry into World War I in 1917 brought him back into politics. He and the Socialist Democratic party denounced U.S. participation in the war. At a state convention of the party in Canton, Ohio, Debs condemned the government of Woodrow Wilson for passing and using a sedition act to prosecute people who spoke out against the administration's war policy and the war generally. He was himself charged with violating the Sedition Act, convicted, and

[35] Eugene V. Debs, "The Outlook for Socialism in the United States," *International Socialist Review* 1 (September 1900): 132–133.

sentenced to a ten-year term in federal prison. As prisoner Number 2253 in the Atlanta Penitentiary, Debs was nominated for president again in 1920; he received 919,799 votes, the largest socialist vote in United States history. He was pardoned a year after the election by the successful Republican candidate, Warren G. Harding, and died in 1926 at the age of seventy-one.

Never an intellectual, Debs was a passionate speaker whose personal popularity made him a leader of the socialist movement and won him love and respect from millions of Americans. Despite much radical rhetoric, he was one of the moderate leaders of socialism in the United States. Unlike many radicals, he not only opposed the use of violence but was also a devout Christian. Ralph Chaplin, the author of *Solidarity Forever*, wrote that "Gene Debs was one of the radicals who could mention God's name on a public platform and get away with it."[36] Although politics became his major interest after the disruption of the American Railway Union, Debs remained active in the labor movement and was a constant critic of Samuel Gompers and craft unionism. He considered craft unionism outdated and advocated instead the formation of industrial unions—unions formed on an industry-wide basis to include all workers in that industry. This, Debs believed, was the only kind of organization that could protect the workers.

The Wobblies—Industrial Workers of the World

"The labor men are very ugly and no one can tell how far such discontent will spread," wrote President Theodore Roosevelt in 1906.

> There has been during the last six or seven years a growth of socialistic and radical spirit among the workingmen and the leaders are obliged to play this or they will lose their leadership.[37]

[36] Quoted in Robert K. Murray, *Red Scare: A Study of National Hysteria, 1919–1920* (New York: McGraw-Hill, 1964), p. 25.

[37] Quoted in Dulles, *Labor in America*, p. 208.

Spearheading this radical movement—which was hardly typical of American labor and not nearly so widespread as some men chose to believe—was the Industrial Workers of the World, formed in Chicago in 1905.

The Wobblies, as they soon came to be called, were concerned primarily with the unorganized and the hitherto unorganizable—principally miners, lumberjacks, and migrant laborers in the West. Socialistic ideas were very important to the Wobblies, even though the strike was their main tactical weapon, and higher wages and better working conditions, especially for unskilled workers, were their immediate goals. As Foster Rhea Dulles has noted:

IWW members demonstrating outside a prison where three of their leaders were being held.

Culver Pictures

> Instead of the conservative motto, "A fair day's wage for a fair day's work," their ringing manifesto declared, "We must inscribe on our banner the revolutionary watchword, 'Abolition of the wage system.' It is the historic mission of the working class to do away with capitalism."[38]

And as "Big Bill" Haywood, the IWW leader, proclaimed, "We are going down in the gutter — among the bums and the working stiffs — to get the mass of workers and bring them up to a decent plane of living."[39]

Given the militancy of the IWW, and given the deep-seated fear of socialist revolution among capitalists, employers, and the general public, it is not surprising that wherever Wobblies went violence was seldom far behind. Frequently Wobbly–employer clashes followed the pattern set by the Western Federation of Miners at Cripple Creek, Colorado, in 1903–1904. During a long strike there, union miners fought strikebreakers, vigilantes, and state militia with equal ferocity. Trains were wrecked, people were murdered, and mines were dynamited. After thirteen months of battle, the mine owners broke the strike.

This defeat pushed the Western Federation of Miners into the IWW when it formed the following year, but the

[38] Ibid., p. 209.

[39] Quoted in ibid., p. 211.

union did not remain there long. Individualism was rampant in the IWW and so was factionalism. Although on paper the IWW was an umbrella organization for various unions, in actuality it was a collection of towering giants of individuals who agreed on socialist goals but were almost constantly at odds about which path to travel to attain them. Many Wobbly leaders occupy prominent and hallowed places in the lore of American militant left-wing unionism. Outsized, one-eyed "Big Bill" Haywood—cowboy, miner, homesteader, and indefatigable socialist organizer—was one. Daniel De Leon, whose speeches and writings in the cause of labor and socialism earned him the nickname "the Socialist Pope," was another. There was also a Reverend T. J. Hagerty, an oversized, black-bearded Catholic priest who edited the American Labor Union's official periodical, and Mother Jones who, well into her seventies, was without peer as a labor agitator. In 1907, after continual bickering, the Western Federation of Miners withdrew from the quarrelsome fold, although Haywood, one of its leaders, remained. The union's defection reduced IWW membership to 6,000. At its peak, the IWW probably had no more than 60,000 members, and most of these had tended to float in and out.

Culver Pictures

"Big Bill" Haywood.

In 1907, the IWW's leaders resolved the issue of whether the organization should focus its efforts on political or economic action. The latter course won. Sang the Wobblies, "Tie 'Em Up!"

We have no fight with brothers of the old A. F. of L.
But we ask you to use your reason with the facts we have
  to tell.
Your craft is but protection from a form of property.
The skill that you are losing, don't you see?
Improvements on machinery take your skill and tools away.
And you'll be among the common slaves upon some
  fateful day.
Now the things of which we're talking we are mighty
  sure about—

So what's the use to strike the way you can't win out?
Tie 'em up! tie 'em up; that's the way to win.
Don't notify the bosses till hostilities begin.
Don't furnish chance for gunmen, scabs and all their like.
What you need is One Big Union and One Big Strike.[40]

The overthrow of capitalism and the placement of the means of production in the hands of workers remained the shining goal.

Although the main Wobbly appeal was to harvest hands, lumberjacks, miners, and construction gangs in the West, the IWW won its greatest victory in the East, for textile workers in Lawrence, Massachusetts.

Economically, 1912 was a good year, especially in the textile industry. Still, the American Woolen Company and other firms in Lawrence cut the wages of their mill hands—mostly Poles, Italians, Lithuanians, and Russians—below the nine dollars a week they had been averaging. At the same time the companies introduced a premium system for piece work; the system was designed to speed up production but instead resulted in tension and turmoil. On January 12, the workers walked out, spontaneously.

Observing the situation as it developed, IWW leaders had anticipated this possibility, and Joseph J. Ettor and Arturo Giovannetti, outstanding Wobbly organizers, were quickly on their way to Lawrence to guide and conduct the strike. They did an excellent job, the Wobblies this time carefully avoiding violence. Organizing mass meetings to keep up morale, setting up picket lines, and arranging for relief for strikers and their families—about half the city's population of 85,000—Ettor and Giovannetti maintained discipline and striker unity.

Then a local antilabor undertaker, seeking to discredit the strike and the IWW, planted dynamite at various places in the city. The dynamite was discovered, and the IWW was immediately blamed. But when the truth of the dynamite's origin was uncovered and the president of the American Woolen Company implicated in the plot, public sentiment swung to the strikers' side.

Next the American Woolen Company attempted to

[40] Quoted in ibid., p. 222.

reopen its plants. Violence between police and strikers resulted, and an Italian woman was shot and killed. Twenty-two militia companies were called in and Ettor and Giovannetti were arrested as accessories to murder.

Still, the IWW instigated no counterviolence. Bill Haywood took over for the jailed leaders. Few strikers accepted a company invitation to return to work under militia protection.

Brown Brothers

The textile workers' strike at Lawrence, Massachusetts.

Now, however, the problem of feeding strikers and their dependents became acute. Money was running out. Haywood and other strike leaders finally hit on the plan of finding labor sympathizers in other cities who would temporarily take in the Lawrence strikers' children, and several hundred children were sent to other communities. Lawrence city authorities denounced this practice and ordered that no more children were to leave the city. The police intervened when another group was about to depart. The railroad station, said one report of what followed,

> was surrounded by police and militia. . . . When the time approached to depart, the children, arranged in a long line, two by two, in orderly procession, with their parents near at hand, were about to make their way to the train when the police, who had by that time stationed themselves along both sides of the door, closed in on us with their clubs, beating right and left, with no thought of the children, who were in the most desperate danger of being trampled to death. The mothers and children were thus hurled in a mass and bodily dragged to a military truck, and even then clubbed, irrespective of the cries of panic-stricken women and children.[41]

This episode won the strike for the IWW and the textile workers. Public outcry was so loud and intense that the American Woolen Company finally caved in and in March met nearly all the strikers' demands. Workers received pay increases of from five to twenty-five percent, time-and-a-quarter for overtime, adjustments in the piece-work premium system, and no discrimination against strike leaders in rehiring. Later, Ettor and Giovannetti were tried and acquitted.

[41] Quoted in ibid., pp. 217–218.

Success at Lawrence rocketed IWW membership to 18,000, but this proved to be the high point in the organization's history. The next year, 1913, the Wobblies lost a five-month strike against silk mills in Paterson, New Jersey, defeated by the mill owners' use of force. After that, the IWW's fortunes fluctuated. The emotionalism and suppression of dissent that followed the United States' entry into World War I finally did the Wobblies in. As socialists, IWW leaders denounced the conflict as a capitalists' war and spoke out strongly against U.S. participation in it. Under federal sedition and espionage acts, and under state criminal syndicalism legislation that outlawed the IWW, Wobbly leaders were arrested and prosecuted for conspiracy, sedition, and treason. "Big Bill" Haywood and ninety-four others were convicted of sedition in a mass trial in Chicago—where emotionalism rather than hard legal proof played the major role—and sentenced to up to twenty years in prison. Local vigilante committees also took a hand in stamping out the Wobblies—clubbings, whippings, and tar-and-feather parties being the favored means of discouraging them and their ideas. In 1917, a group of strikers in Bisbee, Arizona, were driven from the town and forced to survive as best they could in the desert. Without its leaders, the organization began to fall apart. It never recovered its prewar strength, and, as Foster Rhea Dulles has said, "By the mid-1920's the old fighting IWW had already become a legend."[42]

The membership certificate of the United Mine Workers listed eleven demands for better working conditions, such as the eight-hour day, and bore the union's motto, "Labor As Wide As the Earth Has Its Summit in Heaven."

The New York Historical Society

At the End of an Era

From the unionist point of view, there were few bright spots in the American labor picture up to the end of World War I. Probably the most significant victory occurred in 1902. That year, under the leadership of their president, John Mitchell, United Mine Workers in the Pennsylvania coal fields struck for higher pay, an eight-hour day, better safety conditions in the mines, and recognition of the union as the workers' bargaining agent. Samuel Gompers was willing to aid an AFL affiliate and responded to requests

[42] Ibid., p. 222.

The New York Public Library

John Mitchell of the United Mine Workers and his staff.

for relief money for strikers and their families; he also helped Mitchell publicize the union's side of the conflict. After the strike had dragged on for several weeks, Mitchell offered to settle for arbitration, but the mine owners refused to have anything to do with the union.

In the meantime, the nation's coal supplies were running low and winter was coming on. In mid-fall of 1902, President Theodore Roosevelt finally called mine owners and union leaders to the White House and asked them to accept arbitration. The mine owners refused, despite Roosevelt's anger at their unwillingness to compromise. Roosevelt then proceeded to get at them through the back door, persuading J. P. Morgan—whose bank had financed the owners and their mines—that public hostility against the owners was growing and that he had better put pressure on them to settle. Morgan did. Arbitration awarded the miners a ten-percent increase in pay, a nine-hour day, and some provisions for mine safety. For the first time, the power of the federal government had been used on behalf of labor, not management, a fact which alone makes the United Mine Workers' strike of 1902 worthy of remark.

On the whole, however, government functioned in support of industrial owners and managers. Interestingly enough, however, this did not turn droves of workers to embrace socialism or later communism as a means of getting a better deal. The American workingman—unlike so many of his European counterparts—remained essentially conservative; he was not sympathetic to the idea of class struggle or radical redistribution of wealth and power. All that was somehow "foreign." "In reality," wrote Robert K. Murray, the American workingman's movement "was a protest against the conservative craft unionism of the AFL and a defense in behalf of industrial unionism."[43] Like his bosses, he believed in the American dream, believed that the road to success lay open, and believed that one could travel this road by hard work, thrift, and perseverance and achieve success if not for oneself then certainly, in America, for one's children. He did not wish to destroy or even change the system much; he merely wanted a larger slice of the economic pie.

The IWW and other radical labor movements failed because their ideas did not appeal to this basically conservative labor force. Yet, despite its failure and its radical elements, the IWW made a number of important contributions to the American labor scene. The Wobblies publicized the plight of unskilled workers as no other union had done. They gave a great impetus to the cause of industrial unionism; their methods of organizing workers on an industry-wide basis would be used again later and more successfully. But perhaps their most important contribution was the spiritual heritage they created for American labor. Their struggles and sufferings assumed epic proportions in folk song and story, and many of their leaders became martyrs of the labor cause—Frank Little, who was lynched in Butte, Montana; Wesley Everett, who was killed by a group of American Legionnaires in Centralia, Washington; and Joe Hill, a union organizer and songwriter who was executed by the state of Utah for murder even though millions of

[43] Murray, *Red Scare*, p. 27.

people refused to believe that he was guilty. Songs by and about Joe Hill are still sung today.

Of the many labor organizations formed during the late nineteenth century, it was the American Federation of Labor and the craft unions affiliated with it that survived and prospered best. On the whole, the AFL was conservative in its organization and ambitions, and Samuel Gompers used conservative methods to further his goals—he avoided, for example, long struggles that would strain the AFL financially, even though this meant that many strikers had to give in to management without achieving any of their demands. Over the years the AFL did improve the lot of its members, skilled workers sometimes called "the aristocrats of labor," but it was not until the 1930's that unionism, especially among the unskilled, began really to succeed and workers began to receive a larger share of the nation's wealth. By then laissez faire, the commodity theory of labor, and American business as a whole were generally in ill-repute.

SUGGESTED READINGS

Altgeld, John Peter. *The Mind and Spirit of John Peter Altgeld: Selected Writings and Addresses.* Edited by H. M. Christman. University of Illinois Press.

Dulles, Foster Rhea. *Labor in America: A History.* Thomas Y. Crowell.

Foner, Philip S. *The Case of Joe Hill.* International Publishers, New World Paperbacks.

Haywood, William. *The Autobiography of Big Bill Haywood.* International Publishers, New World Paperbacks.

Hill, Joe. *The Letters of Joe Hill.* Edited by Philip S. Foner. Oak Publications.

Iman, Raymond S., and Koch, Thomas W. *Labor in American Society.* Scott, Foresman.

Litwack, Leon, ed. *The American Labor Movement.* Prentice-Hall, Spectrum Books.

Pelling, Henry. *American Labor.* University of Chicago Press.

Renshaw, Patrick. *The Wobblies: The Story of Syndicalism in the United States.* Doubleday, Anchor Books.

The New York Public Library

"The End of the Poor," a drawing published in 1865 showing the unceremonious removal of someone who has died in a tenement on Baxter Street in the Five Points district of New York City.

URBANIZATION

In 1910, fifty American cities had populations of over 100,000 compared with only nine such cities in 1860. In the East, New York and Philadelphia had long since passed the million mark, while midwestern cities such as St. Louis, Cleveland, and Detroit experienced tremendous increases in population. Chicago grew faster than any other city in the nation. In 1860 its population numbered 109,620; by 1910 it had increased to 2,185,283, making the city on Lake Michigan the second largest in the country. New York, wrote Arthur M. Schlesinger,

> was a city of contradiction, reminding one visitor of "a lady in ball costume, with diamonds in her ears, with her toes out at her boots." Against the splendors of Fifth Avenue and the show places of the metropolis had to be sèt the rocky wastes of Shantytown, extending during the 1880's along the East Side from Forty-second to One Hundred and Tenth Street and inhabited by Irish squatters, goats and pigs living promiscuously together. Contrasting with the pillared citadels of wealth in Wall Street was the near-by slum section, a festering spot of poverty and immorality, finding a tawdry outlet for its life in the notorious Bowery.[1]

Chicago, on the other hand, was called "the most American of American cities and yet the most mongrel." It had been quickly rebuilt after the disastrous fire of 1871 and had become once again a thriving metropolis. Said Schlesinger:

> Its business and shopping district, rivaling New York's in high buildings, noise and impressiveness, was fringed by

[1] Arthur M. Schlesinger, *The Rise of the City, 1878–1898* (New York: Macmillan Co., 1933), p. 84,

> three residential areas: the north side, its broad streets lined with handsome abodes, churches and club houses overlooking the lake; the south side, a newer and hardly less aristocratic section, studded with stately mansions and spacious parks; and the vast west side, more populous than the other two combined, where dwelt the immigrants and laboring folk. Like every other great city, Chicago offered a study in contrasts: squalor matching splendor, municipal boodle contending with civic spirit; the very air now reeking with the foul stench of the stockyards, now fresh-blown from prairie or lake. A "splendid chaos" indeed, causing the roving [Rudyard] Kipling to exclaim, "Having seen it, I urgently desire never to see it again."[2]

As one man said about Chicago in 1895:

> This town of ours is the only great city in the world to which all its citizens have come for the common avowed object of making money. There you have its genesis, its growth, its end and object; and there are but few of us who are not attending to that object very strictly. In this Garden City of ours everyone cultivates his own little bed and his neighbor his; but who looks after the paths between? They have become a kind of No Man's Land and the weeds of rank iniquity are fast choking them up.[3]

Thousands of Irishmen came to the United States after disease destroyed Ireland's potato crops in the 1840's. This 1854 cartoon of a Dubliner reading a steamship notice reflects the stereotyped view of the Irish immigrant held by many native Americans.

The New York Historical Society

Immigrants

Great numbers of city dwellers at the turn of the century had been born in rural areas. No longer needed on farms now increasingly mechanized, they were attracted to cities by the jobs that industrialism created. Immigrants, mainly from the cities and towns of Europe, came in even greater numbers. These people had been forced from their homes by poverty, political and religious repression, and lack of economic opportunity; they were hopeful that the streets of America really were cobblestoned with gold nuggets. Scarcely twenty percent of Europeans seeking a better life

[2] Ibid., p. 86.

[3] Quoted in Thomas C. Cochran and William Miller, *The Age of Enterprise* (New York: Harper & Row, Torchbooks, 1961), p. 249.

in the New World settled on farms; the vast majority headed for the cities.

Those who came after 1880 were called "new" immigrants; these "new" people came from southern and eastern Europe, rather than from western and northern Europe as had the "older" immigrants. The huge influx of Italians, Greeks, Croatians, Poles, Russians, and others alarmed some people. Clannish, tending to cling to old country ways and to settle in communities within communities, they did not seem as thrifty, as industrious, or as likely to be beneficial to America as the Germans, Swedes, and others who had made up the bulk of earlier immigration. And, unlike the majority of the earlier immigrants, they were not Protestant; their Jewish, Roman Catholic, and Eastern Orthodox faiths were regarded as "foreign" and somehow threatening by many people. Madison Grant expressed the attitude of more than a few Americans when he wrote:

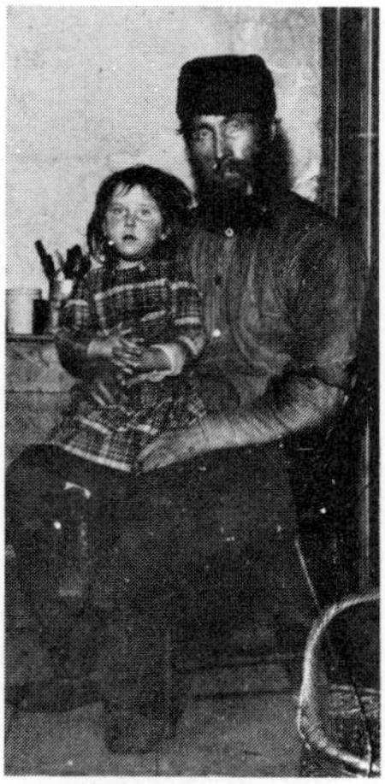

Library of Congress

In 1888 Jacob Riis photographed this father and child in New York City's "Poverty Gap," a slum district where many of the "new" immigrants from eastern Europe were forced to live.

> These new immigrants were no longer exclusively members of the Nordic race as were the earlier ones who came of their own impulse to improve their social conditions. The transportation lines advertised America as a land flowing with milk and honey and the European governments took the opportunity to unload upon the careless, wealthy and hospitable America the sweepings of their jails and asylums. The result was that the new immigration, . . . contained a large and increasing number of the weak, the broken and the mentally crippled of all races drawn from the lowest stratum of the Mediterranean basin and the Balkans, together with hordes of the wretched, submerged populations of the Polish ghettos. Our jails, insane asylums and almshouses are filled with this human flotsam and the whole tone of American life, social, moral and political, has been lowered and vulgarized by them.[4]

Another writer, Francis Walker, expressed the fear that if immigration was not restricted "these Huns, and Poles, and Bohemians, and Russian Jews, and South Italians will con-

[4] Madison Grant, *The Passing of the Great Race* (New York: Charles Scribner's Sons, 1918), pp. 89–90.

tinue to come, and to come by millions." Walker had doubts that these new foreigners would make good citizens:

> Only a small part of these new-comers can read, while the general intelligence of the mass is even below what might be assumed from such a statement. By far the greater part of them are wholly ignorant of our institutions, and, too often, having been brought up in an atmosphere of pure force, they have no sympathy with the political ideas and sentiments which underlie our social organization; often not even the capability of understanding them.[5]

This kind of thinking eventually led to Oriental exclusion laws and to quota laws restricting European immigration.

Threat to the American way of life or not, the new arrivals found no land of milk and honey. They found instead the harsh, smelly, unhealthful reality of the urban slum. The famous Chicago social worker, Jane Addams, wrote:

Brown Brothers

Jane Addams devoted over forty years to social reform work, beginning with the founding of Hull House in Chicago in 1889. In 1931 she received the Nobel Peace Prize for her efforts on behalf of the poor.

> The streets are inexpressibly dirty, the number of schools inadequate, sanitary legislation unenforced, street lighting bad, the paving miserable and altogether lacking in the alleys and smaller streets, and the stables foul beyond description. Hundreds of houses are unconnected with the street sewer. The older and richer inhabitants seem anxious to move away as rapidly as they can afford it. They leave room for newly arrived imigrants.[6]

Migration to the suburbs began as early as the 1880's. Native Americans made room for the Irish and the Germans, and they in turn made room for Poles, Italians, and Jews. Later these groups would give way to Negroes.

Many immigrants found jobs not in factories, but in tenement sweatshops. These small operations, typical of the New York garment district, were frequently overseen by recently arrived immigrants who put their families and others to laboring at piece work making clothes. Writer Jacob Riis described one such sweatshop:

[5] Francis A. Walker, "Immigration and Degradation," *The Forum* 11 (November 1891): 643.

[6] Jane Addams, *Twenty Years at Hull House* (New York: Macmillan Co., 1924), p. 98.

> On the next floor, in a dimly lighted room with a big red-hot stove to keep the pressing irons ready for use, is a family of man, wife, three children, and a boarder. "Knee-pants" are made there too, of a still lower grade. Three cents and a half is all he clears, says the man, and lies probably out of at least two cents. The wife makes a dollar and a half finishing, the man about nine dollars at the machine. The boarder pays sixty-five cents a week. He is really only a lodger, getting his meals outside. The rent is two dollars and twenty-five cents a week, cost of living five dollars. Every floor has at least two, sometimes four, such shops. Here is one with a young family for which life is bright with promise. Husband and wife work together; just now the latter, a comely young woman, is eating her dinner of dry bread and green pickles. Pickles are favorite food in Jewtown. They are filling, and keep the children from crying with hunger. Those who have stomachs like ostriches thrive in spite of them and grow strong—plain proof that they are good to eat. The rest? "Well, they die," says our guide, dryly. No thought of untimely death comes to disturb this family with life all before it. In a few years the man will be a prosperous sweater [sweatshop operator]. Already he employs an old man as ironer at three dollars a week, and a sweet-faced little Italian girl as finisher at a dollar and a half. She is twelve, she says, and can neither read nor write; will probably never learn. How should she? The family clears from ten to eleven dollars a week in brisk times, more than half of which goes into the bank.[7]

In describing another sweatshop, Riis gave more details concerning working conditions and pay:

> Up two flights of dark stairs, three, four, with new smells of cabbage, of onions, of frying fish, on every landing, whirring sewing machines behind closed doors betraying what goes on within, to the door that opens to admit the bundle and the man. A sweater this, in a small way. Five men and a woman, two young girls, not fifteen, and a boy

[7] Jacob A. Riis, *How the Other Half Lives* (New York: Hill & Wang, 1957), pp. 94–95.

who says unasked that he is fifteen, and lies in saying it, are at the machines sewing knickerbockers, "knee-pants" in the Ludlow Street dialect. The floor is littered ankle-deep with half-sewn garments. In the alcove, on a couch of many dozens of "pants" ready for the finisher, a bare-legged baby with pinched face is asleep. A fence of piled-up clothing keeps him from rolling off on the floor. The faces, hands, and arms to the elbows of everyone in the room are black with the color of the cloth on which they are working. The boy and the woman alone look up at our entrance. The girls shoot sidelong glances, but at a warning look from the man with the bundle they tread their machines more energetically than ever. The men do not appear to be aware even of the presence of the stranger.

They are "learners," all of them, says the woman, who proves to be the wife of the boss, and have "come over" only a few weeks ago. She is disinclined to talk at first, but a few words in her own tongue from our guide set her fears, whatever they are, at rest, and she grows almost talkative. The learners work for week's wages, she says. How much do they earn? She shrugs her shoulders with an expressive gesture. The workers themselves, asked in their own tongue, say indifferently, as though the question were of no interest: from two to five dollars. The children—there are four of them—are not old enough to work. The oldest is only six. They turn out one hundred and twenty dozen "knee-pants" a week, for which the manufacturer pays seventy cents a dozen. Five cents a dozen is the clear profit, but her own and her husband's work brings the family earnings up to twenty-five dollars a week, when they have work all the time. But often half the time is put in looking for it. They work no longer than to nine o'clock at night, from daybreak. There are ten machines in the room; six are hired at two dollars a month. For the two shabby, smoke-begrimed rooms, one somewhat larger than ordinary, they pay twenty dollars a month. She does not complain, though "times are not what they were, and it costs a good deal to live." Eight dollars a week for the family of six and two boarders. How do they do it?[8]

[8] Ibid., pp. 92–93.

Library of Congress

A sweatshop on Ludlow Street, photographed by Jacob Riis in 1889.

In New York many immigrants found homes in "dumb-bell" apartments, for twenty years after 1880 virtually the only kind of tenement erected in the city. The name derived from the shape of the building as seen from above, an indentation on each side providing an air and light shaft. Five to six stories high, "dumb bells" ran ninety feet back from the street, with a dark hallway less than three feet wide running through the center. Each floor was a honeycomb of rooms, most without direct light or air. When first built, huge tenements were considered to be an architectural advance; but they soon became grimy, foul-smelling, infested with rats and vermin, and productive of all kinds of diseases. In 1879 the total number of tenements in New York was estimated at 21,000; these tenements were inhabited by half a million people. Ten years later there were 32,000 buildings housing a million people. Within another ten years the number of buildings had risen to 43,000 and their population to 1.5 million people. Arthur M. Schlesinger wrote,

> The dense slum district bounded by Cherry, Catherine, Hamilton and Market streets was known as "lung block" because of the many deaths from tuberculosis. No wonder such rookeries were nurseries of immorality, drunkenness, disease and crime. The real surprise is, as the state tenement-house commission pointed out in 1900, that so many of the children grew up to be decent, self-respecting citizens.[9]

Thousands of children roamed the streets, apparently without homes, sleeping in alleys, in doorways, and on stairs. Jacob Riis told about one:

Riis photographed these "street arabs" —homeless children —on Mulberry Street in New York City about 1890.

Photograph by Jacob A. Riis
The Jacob A. Riis Collection
Museum of the City of New York

> A little fellow who seemed clad in but a single rag was among the flotsam and jetsam stranded at Police Headquarters one day last summer. No one knew where he came from or where he belonged. The boy himself knew as little about it as anybody, and was the least anxious to have light shed on the subject after he had spent a night in the matron's nursery. The discovery that beds were provided for boys to sleep in there, and that he could have "a whole egg" and three slices of bread for breakfast put him on the best of terms with the world in general, and he decided that Headquarters was "a bully place." He sang "McGinty" all through, with Tenth Avenue variations, for the police, and then settled down to the serious business of giving an account of himself. The examination went on after this fashion:
>
> "Where do you go to church, my boy?"
>
> "We don't have no clothes to go to church." And indeed his appearance, as he was, in the door of any New York church would have caused a sensation.
>
> "Well, where do you go to school, then?"
>
> "I don't go to school," with a snort of contempt.

[9] Schlesinger, *Rise of the City*, p. 109.

> "Where do you buy your bread?"
>
> "We don't buy no bread; we buy beer," said the boy, and it was eventually the saloon that led the police as a landmark to his "home." It was worthy of the boy. As he had said, his only bed was a heap of dirty straw on the floor, his daily diet a crust in the morning, nothing else.[10]

Blacks in the Cities

Blacks joined the tide of rural people moving to cities, particularly to the northern cities, lured there by the chance for jobs and the hope of living in a more open society than the one they had known in the Jim Crow South. But most found only menial jobs; labor unions would not admit them, and many employers would not hire them, claiming that they were lazy and inefficient. Nearly all were forced to live under segregated conditions. Even worse was the constant threat of violence. This was especially true in the South, where 1,700 blacks were lynched between 1885 and 1894 alone, but violence occurred all too frequently in the North as well. One of the worst riots occurred in Springfield, Illinois, in 1908, when two blacks were lynched and many were injured. The historian John Hope Franklin has written:

> All of the ills usually associated with maladjustment in urban life arose from the unfavorable conditions which existed among Negroes in American cities, both North and South. Juvenile delinquency became rampant as slum areas grew steadily worse and as too few corrective measures were taken by either public agencies or private individuals. The parks and playgrounds movement that was developing throughout the country early in the century did little for the Negro; and when he attempted to avail himself of the opportunity to use public recreational facilities, violence and bloodshed frequently resulted. Family disorganization and disintegration were a logical consequence of the innumerable difficulties which Negroes faced, and although the church was assuming a greater responsibility, problems increased far more rapidly than it could solve

[10] Riis, *How the Other Half Lives*, pp. 138–139.

> them. The twentieth century, which had opened with such a note of optimism, very early revealed overtones of despair that equaled, if they did not surpass, any which the Negro had experienced.[11]

Still, Negroes continued to migrate from the South, frequently urged to do so by black northern newspapers such as the *Chicago Defender*, which editorialized in 1917:

> To die from the bite of frost is far more glorious than at the hands of a mob. . . . You are a free man. Show the world that you will not let false leaders lead you. Your neck has been in the yoke. Will you continue to keep it there because some "white folks' nigger" wants you to? . . . Get out of the South. Your being there in the numbers in which you are gives the southern politician too strong a hold on your progress. . . . So much has been said through the white papers in the South about the members of the race freezing to death in the North. They freeze to death down South when they don't take care of themselves. There is no reason for any human being staying in the Southland on this bugaboo handed out by the white press.
>
> If you can freeze to death in the North and be free, why freeze to death in the South and be a slave, where your mother, sister and daughter are raped and burned at the stake; where your father, brother and sons are treated with contempt and hung to a pole, riddled with bullets at the least mention that he does not like the way he is treated. Come North then, all you folks. . . . The *Defender* says come.[12]

Harlem, centered around 125th Street in New York City, eventually became the best-known black community in the North. As late as the 1820's few people lived in Harlem; it was still a small village in a country setting. It began to grow in the 1880's, after elevated railroad lines were extended to connect it with lower Manhattan Island,

[11] John Hope Franklin, *From Slavery to Freedom: A History of Negro Americans* (New York: Alfred A. Knopf, 1969), p. 437.

[12] Quoted in Alan Shipiro, Charles McCrea, and Vera Beck, *Black* (Chicago: Science Research Associates, 1970), pp. 64–65.

and many well-to-do families moved to Harlem brownstones and apartment buildings. At the same time a sprinkling of Irish, Italians, Jews, and blacks settled in or near the community.

As the twentieth century opened, most New York Negroes lived in the very crowded midtown section of Manhattan, in dilapidated boarding houses. In August, 1900, a race riot occurred in that part of the city following the stabbing of a policeman by a young black man who claimed that a policeman had been molesting his girlfriend. The riot and the diminishing real estate boom in Harlem gave a black real estate agent, Philip A. Payton, Jr., an idea. Payton leased buildings from Harlem owners, guaranteed them a year's rent, and then upped the price to Negroes who wished to move from midtown. The influx of blacks alarmed Harlem whites, who began to move out. By 1914 there were 50,000 blacks in Harlem; during the 1920's the district became practically all Negro as 100,000 whites left, their places filled by an equal number of blacks. Although parts of Harlem remained middle class and even fashionable, much of it became a ghetto of old, dirty, rundown buildings, littered streets, garbage-strewn alleys, and rat-infested stairways.

Rising crime rates among blacks simply reinforced the racial prejudices of most white city residents, but to a contemporary historian, John R. Commons, the statistics reflected not a "natural" predilection toward crime but rather the demoralizing effects of ghetto life:

> The Negro perhaps suffers by way of discrimination in the number of arrests and convictions compared with whites, yet it is significant that in proportion to total numbers the Negro prisoners in the Northern states are nearly twice as many as in the Southern states. Here, again, city life works its degenerating effects, for the Northern Negroes are congregated mainly in towns and cities, while the Southern Negroes remain in the country.[13]

Mortality rates provided another measure of the quality

[13] John R. Commons, *Races and Immigrants in America* (New York: Macmillan Co., 1907), p. 172.

of black ghetto life. To racists and others who wished to keep their consciences clear, the fact that significant numbers of blacks died younger than whites proved the blacks' innate physical inferiority. However, a black physician offered a different explanation:

> Is it any wonder that we die faster than our white brother when he gets the first and best attention, while we are neglected on all sides? They have the best wards and treatment at the hospital, while we must take it second hand or not at all; they have all the homes for the poor and friendless, we have none; they have a home for fallen women, we have none; they have the public libraries where they can get and read books on hygiene and other subjects pertaining to health, we have no such privileges; they have the gymnasiums where they can go and develop themselves physically, we have not; they have all the parks where they and their children can go on the hot summer days and breathe the pure, cool air, but for fear we might catch a breath of that air and live, they put up large signs, which read thus, "For white people only"; they live in the best homes, while we live in humble ones; they live in the cleanest and healthiest parts of the city, while we live in the sickliest and filthiest parts of the city; the streets on which they live are cleaned once and twice a day, the streets on which we live are not cleaned once a month, and some not at all; besides, they have plenty of money with which they can get any physician they wish, any medicine they need, and travel for their health when necessary; all of these blessings we are deprived of. Now, my friends, in the face of all these disadvantages, do you not think we are doing well to stay here as long as we do?[14]

The Urban Middle Class

For the middle class, life in a late nineteenth-century American city was fairly decent. There was money to be made, fine houses and apartment buildings to live in, and plenty of amusements. Robert H. Walker has described a middle-class Sunday in the city:

[14] Quoted in ibid., pp. 58–59.

> Sundays would center on church just as surely if not so extensively in city as in town. Services began later and were attended by packed congregations of very carefully turned-out families who often found the intellectual climax of their week in what was said from the pulpit of the socially conscious urban minister. The morning service would have been lengthy and might have been further attenuated by Sunday School or Bible Class before or after; but evening services, although they were still customarily offered, were not attended so compulsively as they were in small communities. The greatest contrast, however, was between the arrested motion of the strict small-town Sabbath and the bustle of the city corrupted by the "continental Sabbath" of exuberant recreation. This was the day the German immigrants flocked to their beer gardens for music and dancing, setting what many considered a sacrilegious precedent. In the city, however, the prospect of so many people enjoying themselves so thoroughly was too much for even Victorian Puritanism to resist. Soon stores and places of amusement were staying open Sundays, and, except in areas where fundamentalist religious views predominated, the day became one of carefree entertainment, outdoors if possible. There were zoos and amusement parks to be visited; lakes for skating in winter and boating in summer; tennis, baseball, and golf to be played or watched; and fine places to dine.[15]

Yet the urban environment eroded family structure even among the middle class. As Walker has pointed out:

> Although the family was still unquestionably the important social unit, it was beginning to lose the dominance it had enjoyed at midcentury. Girls were no longer spending their afternoons at their mothers' sides during school years, then helping patiently at home until marriage made them housewives themselves. Instead they were finishing high school, even going to college and professional schools, and

[15]Robert H. Walker, *Everyday Life in the Age of Enterprise* (New York: G. P. Putnam's Sons, 1967), p. 244. Reprinted by permission of G. P. Putnam's Sons. Copyright © by Robert H. Walker.

diluting home ties with aims and desires formed and kindled outside. If marriage did not overtake them early, they would leave home anyway to live in boarding houses or small apartments and begin their own careers. Boys exhibited even more independence. A small-town father in the 1860's was doubtless pleased when a well-behaved son came down to the store to learn the trade and follow in his father's footsteps. The urban father of the 1890's hoped that his son would go on to college, enjoy the advantages of an education he himself had probably never known, and display these advantages by surpassing his father in every way. If it is, as some have observed, a trait of American fathers to want their sons to outdo them—grow taller, get better grades in school, attend better colleges, make more money and move in better circles—then the fathers of the 1890's exhibited this trait most emphatically.[16]

Well-to-do Americans in the city spent money on art, although for the most part they preferred foreign painting and sculpture to native productions. Conditions for American novelists, playwrights, and theatrical performers, as Thomas C. Cochran and William Miller have noted, were somewhat more bullish:

> Books or plays were much cheaper than painting or statuary, and as the leisured groups, especially among women, grew in size, they spent more and more time reading and attending the theater in large cities. . . . And as experience with books increased, taste gradually improved and gifted novelists like Hamlin Garland, Frank Norris, Jack London, Stephen Crane, Edith Wharton, and Theodore Dreiser found adequate markets for their works. As the trend toward monopoly led to more and more frequent questioning of the value and validity of traditional American ideals, most of these writers helped maintain a continuous attack upon railroad corporations, investment bankers, great land companies, grain brokers, monopolists of public services. Novels, and to a lesser extent plays, gradually became vehicles of social protest, and as such they attracted many

[16] Ibid., p. 235.

readers or spectators who had no genuine interest in art but were harassed every day by the problems with which literary artists dealt, and to which they seemed to offer solutions.[17]

The City and Its Amusements

People without much interest in the arts or social problems also spent their leisure time at the theater; the theaters they favored featured melodrama, vaudeville, or burlesque. Foster Rhea Dulles has described New York's Bowery Theatre during the 1890's:

> It was a house which combined melodrama and variety for the delectation of [a] rough-and-ready audience. . . . Admission to a box was seventy-five cents, but the gallery

Culver Pictures

In March, 1894, the *Police Gazette* devoted its cover to Fatima and the "danse du ventre," or belly dance, that she performed nightly in Brooklyn, New York.

[17] Cochran and Miller, *Age of Enterprise*, pp. 258–259.

cost only a dime. House policemen endeavored to maintain order. The officer assigned to the parquet [the main floor of the theater] was accustomed to stand throughout the performance with his back to the orchestra leader, a formidable figure with long black mustaches, wearing a derby. Any one who became too noisy would feel the sharp rap of his cane and the hissed warning, "Cheese it!" The theater had a convenient bar. Throughout the show waiters hurried about, and glasses of foaming beer were continually being passed back and forth. . . .

Almost as popular as the melodrama, greatly favored by the lone male in the big city, were the burlesque shows. They had come in shortly after the Civil War, in those wicked days when the cancan was all the rage and English burlesque queens first offered up their "fatted calves at the shrine of a prodigal New York audience." There had been outraged protests against this type of show. Critics almost wept at the public's "porcine taste for indelicate buffoonery," but the managers of the popular theaters knew a good thing, from a strictly commercial point of view, when they saw it. If reformers chose to describe a production as a "disgraceful spectacle of padded legs jigging and wriggling in the insensate follies and indecencies of the hour," it seldom hurt box-office receipts.[18]

For cheap entertainment around the turn of the century there was also the nickelodeon, or nickel movie, then a rather primitive series of soundless, flickering images.

The moving picture inevitably had caustic critics. The nickelodeons were called silly and time-wasting, if not actually pernicious. Anthony Comstock [secretary of the Society for the Suppression of Vice in New York from 1873 to 1915] found in the darkened theaters intimations of immorality which sent anticipatory shivers up his puritanic spine. Censorship was threatened from the day when social reformers in Atlantic City protested the "hypogastric

[18] Foster Rhea Dulles, *A History of Recreation: America Learns to Play,* 2nd ed. (New York: Appleton-Century-Crofts, 1965), p. 217. Copyright © 1965. Reprinted by permission of Appleton-Century-Crofts, Educational Division, Meredith Corporation.

rhythm" of a peep-show depiction of Dolorita's Passion Dance. "The authorities request us not to show the Houchi Kouchi," the exhibitioner sadly wrote the producer, "so please cancel order for new Dolorita. . . ." The kinetoscope's first kiss created a sensation and it was perhaps the editor of a small Chicago magazine, *The Chap Book*, who most forthrightly expressed a widespread disapproval. "In a recent play called The Widow Jones," he wrote, "you may remember a famous kiss, which Miss May Irwin bestowed on a certain John C. Rice, and *vice versa.* Neither participant is physically attractive, and the spectacle of their prolonged pasturing on each other's lips was hard to bear. When only life size it was pronounced beastly. Magnified to Gargantuan proportions and repeated three times over it is absolutely disgusting. . . . Such things call for police interference."[19]

But theaters and movies were comparatively innocent when measured against some of the other amusements the city had to offer:

> Dime museums, dance-halls, shooting-galleries, beer-gardens, bowling-alleys, billiard-parlors, saloons, and other more questionable resorts made up another whole world of entertainment whose glaring gas-lights symbolized the lure of the wicked city. And in the 1890's it often was wicked. It was an age of notoriously corrupt municipal governments. The line between virtue and vice was hard to distinguish; perfectly respectable places of entertainment shaded off imperceptibly into notorious dives. There were plenty of dance-halls that found "the young mechanics and dressmakers in their glory," but as many where the floor was crowded with prostitutes. Every large city had its red-light district given over to saloons and sporting-houses. Drinking, gambling, and prostitution had become tremendous social problems as the size of the constantly growing cities made control more and more difficult, particularly where politics formed its profitable alliance with vice.[20]

[19] Ibid., p. 290.
[20] Ibid., p. 220.

Spectator sports offered a healthier form of entertainment. By the 1890's baseball was using most of the rules, equipment, and techniques of the present-day game, and it was so popular that it was already known as America's "national sport." Horse races and trotting matches drew large crowds to newly constructed tracks near the urban areas. Rowing matches were much more popular then than they are now and also drew large crowds. Boxing was perhaps a less healthy interest, for at that time the contestants wore no gloves and had at each other with bare fists.

> If there was a rival to the national game in sustained popular interest, it was prize-fighting, not wholly out from under the cloud of disapproval but nevertheless arousing a nation-wide excitement which official bans on championship bouts in no way diminished. The fortunes of favorite bruisers were followed avidly, and although it was still true that comparatively few people actually saw the fights, the reports of them were read by millions. An English visitor was somewhat shocked that his newspaper one morning in 1892 gave twelve prominent columns to a championship bout while the death of John Greenleaf Whittier rated only a single inside column. But it was a correct appraisal of public interest.
>
> The great event of the prize-fight world was the emergence of a champion of champions who dominated the ring from 1882 to 1892. America had perhaps never had a sports hero comparable to John L. Sullivan, the Strong Boy of Boston. He climbed to eminence over the prone body of Paddy Ryan, but it was when he knocked out Jake Kilrain in a fierce, grueling, seventy-five-round battle at New Orleans, the last of the bare-knuckle championship fights, that the great John L. was acknowleged lord of all he surveyed. His fame resounded throughout the world after this epic encounter, from which he won a purse of $20,000 and a diamond-studded championship belt presented by *The Police Gazette*.[21]

The late nineteenth century also gave rise to intercol-

[21] Ibid., pp. 226–227.

legiate football, although attendance at games was largely confined to residents of university and college towns. Beginning among the Ivy League schools of the East, college football soon spread to every part of the country. As an adjunct to college life, however, it was not universally welcomed, as Foster Rhea Dulles has noted:

> The preference accorded football-players in their college work, undue absorption in the game through long training-seasons, the prevalent spirit of winning at any cost, and the open hiring of star players awoke a resentment which echoed throughout the country. *The Nation* was foremost in these early onslaughts; it saw all the worst elements of American character reflected in the game. "The spirit of the American youth, as of the American man, is to win, to 'get there,' by fair means or foul," it declared caustically, "and the lack of moral scruple which pervades the business world meets with temptations equally irresistible in the miniature contests of the football field." Although far more sympathetic, the special sports writer of *Harper's Weekly* was fully as outspoken against the rising tide of professionalism. It was prevalent among the eastern colleges, but even worse in other parts of the country. No one could have any conception, Caspar Whitney wrote in 1895, "of the rottenness of the whole structure through the middle and far West. Men are bought and sold like cattle to play this autumn on 'strictly amateur' elevens."[22]

Other Characteristics of the City

Entertainment aside, by 1900 the American city could be characterized in the following ways:

Paved streets. Asphalt, imported from natural beds on the island of Trinidad, was the most common material used, although brick ran a close second. Macadam, a cheaper material made of crushed stone, sufficed for residential streets. By 1900, city governments had laid over 30 million square miles of asphalt alone, but of all the cities Chicago remained an exception. There only about 700 of the total

[22] Ibid., pp. 244–245.

2,048 miles of streets were paved in any fashion—about half with wooden blocks, the remainder with macadam, stone, cinders, or cobblestones.

Incandescent lighting. Arc lights came into being in the 1880's to brighten city streets at night, while interiors of buildings still depended on kerosene, hissing natural gas, and illuminating oil. Thomas Edison got a carbonized cotton thread to glow for forty-five hours inside a vaccum bulb in 1879 and steadily improved his product, patenting an incandescent lamp in 1880. In 1882 both New York and London installed central lighting stations; by 1900 there were about three thousand of them in American cities. One result of better illumination was an extension of production time in mills and factories.

The telephone model in use in 1878, when the world's first commercial switchboard opened in New Haven, Connecticut. The receiver and transmitter were both located in the bottom of the wooden hand-piece; the push-button was used to signal the operator.

American Telephone & Telegraph Company

Telephones. Within a quarter of a century after Alexander Graham Bell completed his work, Americans had become the most talkative people on earth. The telephone quickly passed from the realm of a curious gadget to a business and later a household necessity. In 1880 there were some fifty thousand subscribers to phone service in the nation; ten years later, there were five times that many. By 1900 there were nearly a million phones in use.

Public transportation. Horse-drawn cars and omnibuses gave way to electric street cars, elevated railways, and eventually underground railways. Cable cars also became popular in numerous cities, including hilly San Francisco. Boston built the first subway; New York began work on its subway in 1904.

Water and waste disposal. By the 1890's, most urban middle-class homes had piped-in water. Many homes had small gas-fired water heating tanks in the kitchen and bathroom, but only first-class hotels and the homes of the wealthy had large basement heating tanks with separate systems of hot-water pipes. In a few areas, a household's waste water might drain into a public sewer under the street; more commonly, however, it emptied into a backyard cesspool or septic tank from which the residue was periodically collected and disposed of in some manner.

The efficient disposal of sewage and garbage remained a difficult problem at the end of the nineteenth century.

By the 1850's, Chicago, New York, and Boston had built underground conduits for carrying sewage to nearby bodies of water. Most cities, however, continued to use cesspools and other vault-like methods of storage. Chicago had some thirty thousand of these cesspools in addition to its sewage system; by reversing the flow of the Chicago River from Lake Michigan into the Illinois River, the city increased its means of disposing of waste, although it increased also the amount of pollution to the west and along the Mississippi River. New York and Boston carried garbage on scows and barges out into the Atlantic and dumped it. Many inland cities sold their garbage to farmers for hog feed, although incinerators for disposing of waste by burning were introduced in the 1880's.

There were marked differences among cities with respect to the purity of their water supplies. Between 1880 and 1890 more people died of typhoid in Philadelphia and Chicago—6.8 and 6.25 per 10,000 inhabitants—than in Boston and New York—3.5 and 3.36 respectively. Only 600 cities large and small had public waterworks in 1878, the rest depending entirely on individual wells; by 1900, however, about 3,500 cities had municipal systems.

Crime. As cities grew, so did crime rates and the number of prison inmates. The number of reported homicides rose from 1,266 in 1881, to 4,290 in 1890, to 7,840 in 1898. Suicides, incidentally, increased from 605 to 2,640 to 5,920 in those same years. Most of these violent deaths occurred in cities, and the increase was not entirely related to simple population growth. Cases of personal and bank robbery, swindling, pick-pocketing, and assault showed proportionate increases. Prostitution also grew. According to Arthur M. Schlesinger,

> Primarily an urban phenomenon, [prostitution] throve most extensively in the great population centers where unmarried men congregated in largest numbers and out-of-town visitors were numerous. In New York, for example, vice catered to all tastes and purses—in "palatial bagnios" as well as in widely scattered medium-class houses and places of assignation, not to mention basement dives on the

> Bowery where, we may well believe, the business was "divested of the gaslight glare and tinsel of the high-toned seraglios." As in the seaboard metropolis, "sporting houses" existed in all parts of Chicago, though the traffic was most boldly carried on in the district between Harrison and Polk and between Clark and Division streets. There, as in the red-light districts of other cities, the male passer-by after dark was almost certain to be hailed from curtained windows or accosted on the street by pert sauntering women.[23]

Police forces were professionalized in the nineteenth century, but not all their members were above corruption. All too often police officers were in league with corrupt city politicians. Reformers were able now and then to clean up a city and break the ties that linked grafting politicians to police to criminals, but seldom were the effects lasting.

Governing the Cities

There is only one word for American city government in the nineteenth century: bad. As President Andrew D. White of Cornell University wrote in 1890:

> Without the slightest exaggeration we may assert that, with very few exceptions, the city governments of the United States are the worst in Christendom—the most expensive, the most inefficient, and the most corrupt. No one who has any considerable knowledge of our own country and of other countries can deny this.[24]

The typical American city of the nineteenth century was run by a "boss." He frequently held no political office, but by controlling votes—particularly among immigrants and the poor—he possessed great political power. His "machine," made up of numerous lieutenants and an army of paid workers, controlled the city. "Here," wrote Thomas C. Cochran and William Miller, "was the core of municipal power."

[23] Schlesinger, *Rise of the City*, pp. 156–157.

[24] Andrew D. White, "The Government of American Cities," *The Forum* 10 (December 1890): 357.

> The "boss" was the businessman in politics, the man who set the prices for special favors, sold the franchises, and guaranteed a controlled electorate. He was the man who made it possible to conduct government in the interest of the upper middle class in spite of a great lower-class electorate. He was not unique in the United States. His work was less obvious in England because of his greater respectability and in Germany because of less local democracy. But in English and German cities as well as American, he helped to preserve the established structure of society. Unopposed by well-managed machines and efficient party bosses, the eleven million American families with an average income of $380 a year might well have voted themselves all kinds of remedies, well or ill advised, for their relative poverty. They might also have elected such radicals as Henry George or Eugene Debs to municipal offices. Against the bosses, however, such radicals could get nowhere, and the bosses, for their success in reconciling equality at the polls with inequality in property, were allowed their price in graft. A reform movement might prove worthwhile every now and then to keep the boss in his place, but really to eliminate him was unthinkable.[25]

The reign of William Marcy Tweed in New York City in the 1860's and early 1870's has long been the classic lurid example of expensive, graft-ridden municipal government. Tweed became a symbol of corruption.

William Marcy Tweed began his political career as a leader of one of New York's many volunteer fire departments in the 1840's. In 1852 he ran as the Democratic candidate for alderman in a normally Whig ward, winning the election mainly because he persuaded a friend to run as an independent Whig against the regular party nominee, thus splitting the vote. As a politician Tweed showed promise. "The Common Council to which Tweed was elected," wrote Denis Tilden Lynch, "has gone down in history as the Forty Thieves."

> The position of Alderman in 1852 was one of considerable power. The Alderman was a petty despot. He appointed

[25] Cochran and Miller, *Age of Enterprise*, p. 267.

> the police of his ward, from the humblest patrolman to the commander of the precinct. He granted licenses to saloons, or porter houses, as the language of the day had it. And with his associates, he awarded franchises to operate 'bus and street car lines and ferries. These grants, of course, were not valid until signed by the Mayor, and if disapproved by him, they could be repassed over his veto by the Aldermen. He enjoyed other powers that enabled him—if he were so inclined—to levy blackmail, but these were his principal sources of tainted money. He enjoyed still another privilege. He sat as a Justice in the Mayor's Court, which tribunal, now no more, tried all prisoners accused of violations at the polls.
>
> It was this last which made offenses against the Election Law as safe as dropping money in the collection basket on Sunday. These offenses against the ballot were not confined to any party, so that the political belief of the offender never prejudiced a Justice of the Mayor's Court. Moreover, the Aldermen were practical politicians, who either connived at these frauds or were parties to them. In many cases the Aldermen were the *agents provocateurs* of the offenses brought before them.[26]

Tweed did not remain long on the Common Council. He served a term in Congress in the 1850's but found municipal affairs much more interesting—and profitable—and began to work his way up in Tammany Hall, the New York City Democratic organization. By 1860 he controlled Tammany and was known as Boss Tweed.

Tammany Hall had grown in political power by allying itself with the interests—at least the immediate interests—of the city's poor. The organization supported popular proposals such as the abolition of imprisonment for debt, and it won the loyalty of Irish and other immigrant groups by opposing the various anti-Catholic movements that grew up in response to the influx of immigrants. Tammany distributed food, fuel, and clothing to the poor during times

[26] Denis Tilden Lynch, *"Boss" Tweed, The Story of a Grim Generation* (New York: Boni & Liveright, 1927), p. 67.

of depression, and through the influence of Democratic officeholders the organization was also able to distribute a number of government jobs to its supporters. The U.S. Customs House was Tammany's particular province; most customs employees owed their jobs to Tammany patronage and paid a certain percentage of their salaries to the organization. Tweed did not invent Tammany Hall, corruption in city government, or the boss system, but during his reign he enlarged the operations of all three.

Under Tweed's influence, working through councilmen and mayors, Tammany gave New Yorkers more efficient government and better services than they had ever known. New streets were laid, the park system was expanded, and the transportation system improved. But all this was at a price—a very stiff price. For a time Oakey Hall, a Tweed confederate, was mayor. Peter Sweeny, another associate, was district attorney, then city chamberlain. Still another member of the Tweed Ring was "Slippery Dick" Connolly, the city treasurer. He kept the books. These three men and Tweed, as well as other members of the group, grew rich mainly on kickbacks from contractors and franchise holders who performed services—street cleaning, building streets, laying out parks, and running horsecar lines—for the city. Those who did work for the city could afford to pay kickbacks because Tweed and his men saw to it that they charged in every case much more than the jobs would ordinarily cost. The Tweed Ring also benefited from inside information—from, as Ring member George Washington Plunkett put it, "honest graft." Wrote Plunkett:

> Everybody is talkin' these days about Tammany men growin' rich on graft, but nobody thinks of drawin' the distinction between honest graft and dishonest graft. There's all the difference in the world between the two. . . . I'm gettin' richer every day, but I've not gone in for dishonest graft—blackmailin' gamblers, saloon-keepers, disorderly people, etc.—and neither has any of the men who have made big fortunes in politics.
>
> There's an honest graft, and I'm an example of how it works. I might sum up the whole thing by sayin': "I seen

> my opportunities and I took 'em.". . . My party's in power in the city, and it's goin' to undertake a lot of public improvements. Well, I'm tipped off, say, that they're going to lay out a new park at a certain place.
>
> I see my opportunity and I take it. I go to that place and I buy up all the land I can in the neighborhood. Then the board of this or that makes its plan public, and there is a rush to get my land, which nobody cared particular for before.
>
> Ain't it perfectly honest to charge a good price and make a profit on my investment and foresight? Of course, it is. Well, that's honest graft.[27]

The Ring could always deliver the votes to keep its men in power. Its workers met immigrants at the piers, found them jobs and places to live, helped them quickly become citizens, and aided them in time of need. These services bought voter loyalty. The Ring also used "repeaters" extensively on election days. For a dollar a vote, a repeater voted early and often, each time in a different precinct under a different name. The Ring's political power enabled it to dictate the Democratic nominations for all municipal offices and for many state offices—including the governorship—as well. In 1866, Tweed had himself elected to the New York State Senate.

Perhaps the Tweed Ring's greatest economic triumph was the new county courthouse. Budgeted at $250,000, the building ultimately cost New York taxpayers $12.5 million. Early in the 1870's, *Harper's Weekly*, with powerful anti-Tweed cartoons by Thomas Nast, and the *New York Times* began series of articles on graft and corruption in the city that eventually toppled the Tweed Ring. Reporters relied heavily for material on the books kept by "Slippery Dick" Connolly himself.

> First appeared the armory frauds . . . and then the equally madly extravagant prices for furnishings and labor for the new Court House from January 1, 1869. Andrew J. Garvey, plasterer for The Ring, was paid $138,187 for two days'

[27] Quoted in Alan Shipiro, Charles McCrea, and Vera Beck, *Growth* (Chicago: Science Research Associates, 1970), pp. 49–50.

> work. Garvey, who was called The Prince of Plasterers by *The Times*, had a total bill of $2,870,464.06, which had been paid. Jennings, satirizing the shouted charity of The Ring, suggested Garvey give the odd six cents to the poor. To Tweed's New York Printing Company a single item of stationery netted $186,495.61. Thermometers for the Court House were charged at $7,500. Three tables and forty chairs cost the taxpayers $179,729.60. The firm which supplied this, James H. Ingersoll and Company, whose head was a chairmaker, and a boyhood friend of Tweed's father, received a total of $5,691,144.26 for furniture for this temple of justice. The Ring carpenter, George S. Miller, was paid $360,747.61 for one month's work. Lumber worth $48,000 cost the taxpayers $460,000. John H. Keyser received $1,149,847.50 for repairing plumbing and gas light fixtures in the Court House. His total charges aggregated nearly $3,000,000. All save one of these swindlers were unknown to the people at large. Keyser, The Ring's plumber, was noted for his philanthropy. He was a trustee or director in several charitable organizations.[28]

In 1870 cartoonist Thomas Nast portrayed "Boss Tweed" as being beyond the reach of the law. Although many of his cohorts escaped prosecution, Tweed did not. He served a two-year jail sentence (1873–1875) on Blackwell Island and died in the New York City's Ludlow Street Jail shortly after his extradition from Spain on another charge.

No one knows the total amount the Tweed group stole from the city. It may have been as great as $100 million.

The actual destruction of the Tweed Ring, following the newspaper charges of corruption, came about through the efforts of Samuel J. Tilden, chairman of the Democratic state committee. Tweed was tried, convicted, and imprisoned in 1873; he died in prison in 1878. Tilden was elected governor of New York in 1874 and almost became president of the United States in 1876—he received one less electoral vote than the Republican candidate, Rutherford B. Hayes, after a highly controversial recount of votes.

With Tweed gone, New York City's government became cleaner but less efficient. According to historian Seymour Mandelbaum,

> Unable to build a stable coalition . . . the city marked time in the first half of the eighties as rival factions battled.

[28] Lynch, *"Boss" Tweed*, pp. 364–365.

> Having condemned Tammany for its overweening power, the reformers were unable to construct a new and stable institution in its place. An unstable political structure—a divided society—accommodated rapid change but could not control it. New York . . . was a city committed to the "American idea," a city—a giant—without direction.[29]

Poor city government was not unique to New York. St. Louis, Chicago, Philadelphia, and even Washington, D.C. experienced it too. Early in the twentieth century, a journalist named Lincoln Steffens wrote a series of magazine articles—later published as *The Shame of the Cities*—on municipal graft and corruption. In one article, he examined the causes of this corruption:

> When I set out on my travels, an honest New Yorker told me honestly that I would find that the Irish, the Catholic Irish, were at the bottom of it all everywhere. The first city I went to was St. Louis, a German city. The next was Minneapolis, a Scandinavian city, with a leadership of New Englanders. Then came Pittsburgh, Scotch Presbyterian, and that was what my New York friend was. "Ah, but they are all foreign population," I heard. The next city was Philadelphia, the purest American community of all, and the most hopeless. And after that came Chicago and New York, both mongrel-bred, but the one a triumph of reform, the other the best example of good government that I had seen. The "foreign element" excuse is one of the hypocritical lies that save us from clear sight of ourselves.
>
> Another such conceit of our egotism is that which deplores our politics and lauds our business. This is the wail of the typical American citizen. Now, the typical American citizen is a business man. The typical business man is a bad citizen; he is busy. If he is a "big business man" and very busy, he does not neglect, he is busy with politics, oh, very busy and very businesslike. I found him buying boodlers [offering bribes] in St. Louis, defending grafters in Minneapolis, originating corruption in Pittsburgh, sharing with bosses in Philadelphia, deploring reform in Chicago,

[29] Seymour J. Mandelbaum, *Boss Tweed's New York* (New York: John Wiley & Sons, 1965), p. 181. Reprinted with permission.

> and beating good government with corruption funds in New York. He is a self-righteous fraud, this big business man. He is the chief source of corruption, and it were a boon if he would neglect politics. But it is not the [big] business man who neglects politics; that worthy is the good citizen, the typical business man. He too is busy, he is the one that has no use and therefore no time for politics. When his neglect has permitted bad government to go so far that he can be stirred to action, he is unhappy, and he looks around for a cure that shall be quick, so that he may hurry back to the shop. Naturally, too, when he talks politics, he talks shop. His patent remedy is quack; it is business.
>
> "Give us a business man," he says. . . . "Let him introduce business methods into politics and government; then I shall be left alone to attend to my business."[30]

Steffens pointed out that businessmen had been elected to offices ranging from alderman to United States senator without any noticeable improvement in government. The businessman had failed in politics as much as in citizenship. The reason:

> Because politics is business. That's what's the matter with it. . . .
>
> The commercial spirit is the spirit of profit, not patriotism; of credit, not honor; of individual gain, not national prosperity; of trade and dickering, not principle. "My business is sacred," says the business man in his heart. "Whatever prospers my business, is good; it must be. Whatever hinders it, is wrong. It must be. A bribe is bad, that is, it is a bad thing to take; but it is not so bad to give one, not if it is necessary to my business." "Business is business" is not political sentiment, but our politician has caught it. He takes essentially the same view of the bribe, only he saves his self-respect by piling all his contempt upon the bribe-giver, and he has the great advantage of candor. "It is wrong, maybe," he says, "but if a rich merchant can afford to do business with me for the sake of convenience or to increase his already great wealth, I can afford, for

[30] Lincoln Steffens, *The Shame of the Cities* (New York: Hill & Wang, 1957), p. 2.

> the sake of a living, to meet him half way. I make no pretensions to virtue, not even on Sunday." And as for giving bad government or good, how about the merchant who gives bad goods or good goods, according to the demand?[31]

And there, according to Steffens, lay the crux of the problem. People got the government they demanded. "When I set out to describe the corrupt systems of certain typical cities," wrote Steffens,

> I meant to show simply how the people were deceived and betrayed. But in the very first study—St. Louis—the startling truth lay bare that corruption was not merely political; it was financial, commercial, social; the ramifications of boodle were so complex, various, and far-reaching, that one mind could hardly grasp them. . . .[32]

Reform governments were few and far between, but a few existed. Hazen Pingree of Detroit and Thomas L. Johnson of Cleveland were outstanding examples of reform mayors. Johnson's administration limited the use of franchises for public services—a favorite source of graft—and advocated public ownership of utilities. The key to his support was his insistence on public welfare projects for the poor. Lincoln Steffens considered Cleveland under Johnson's leadership the best-governed city in the nation. Pingree had followed similar policies in Detroit. Detroit was among the first cities to own its electric lighting plant.

Samuel M. "Golden Rule" Jones, mayor of Toledo, Ohio, was rare even among reformers—he was an idealistic socialist. Wrote Jones in 1899:

> Somewhere in God's universe there is such a thing as social justice. Equality *is* as brotherhood *is*. It is not a fad of mere theorists or a whim of dreamers, but a fact from which there is not more possibility of escape than from the facts of arithmetic.[33]

Jones condemned political parties because their members'

[31] Ibid., pp. 4–5.

[32] Ibid., p. 9.

[33] Samuel M. Jones, "The New Patriotism," *Municipal Affairs Magazine* 3 (March 1899): 456–457.

first interest was to govern for the benefit of the party, not the body politic they served. He also had harsh words for the idea of competition: "The competitive idea at present dominant in most of our political and business life is, of course, the seed root of all the trouble." Jones explained his program for municipal socialism in the following way:

> The people are beginning to understand that we have been pursuing a policy of plundering ourselves, that in the foolish scramble to make individuals rich we have been making all poor . . . . It is one of the paradoxes of public opinion that the people of America, least tolerant of this theory of anarchy in political government, lead in practicing it in industry. . . . We are coming to understand that every public utility and necessity to the public welfare should be publicly owned, publicly operated and publicly paid for. Among the properties that according to any scientific conception of the purpose of government should be so owned are water works, heating and lighting plants, street railways, telephones, fire alarms, telegraphs, parks, playgrounds, baths, washhouses, municipal printing establishments, and many other industries necessary to the welfare of the whole family that can only be successfully operated by the family in the interest of the whole family.[34]

Jones, like Pingree and Johnson, gave voice to a growing trend in city government—increased public ownership of utilities and facilities. No city went as far in that direction as Jones wished, but a number eventually adopted public ownership of transportation lines and water systems, and city-operated fire departments became the rule.

Municipal reformers, drawn mainly from the Protestant middle class, generally lacked the common touch and appealed little to the masses of city residents, many of whom were poor and—among immigrants especially—Catholic. Reformers frequently concentrated on changing the form rather than the substance of city government. They campaigned for such things as greater freedom from state government restrictions, nonpartisan elections, and the city manager system of government. These issues held little

[34] Ibid., pp. 460–461.

interest for the working classes, who were concerned first of all with jobs and second with better places in which to live. Bosses provided jobs, they gave handouts to the poor, and they rewarded people directly for voting. The middle-class businessman, as Lincoln Steffens noted, seldom became concerned with corruption unless it began to cost him more in taxes than it helped him in business. Then he was interested only in throwing the rascals out. Reformers often seemed unable to grasp the mechanics of city government, the need to reconcile discordant elements within a metropolis, and the importance of helping the poor with jobs and other services as the bosses had done. Reformers, in short, were seldom good politicians. Perhaps they were too high-minded. As a consequence, in many cities reform governments marked only brief interludes between systems dominated by bosses or political machines. Even today, there are some students of municipal government who wonder if any other form of city government really works as well as the boss system.

In summing up the development of the American city, Arthur M. Schlesinger wrote:

> If we consider only the sordid aspects of urban life the American city of the period seems a cancerous growth. But the record as a whole was distinctly creditable to a generation which found itself confronted with the phenomenon of a great population everywhere clotting into towns. No other people had ever met such an emergency so promptly or, on the whole, so successfully. The basic facilities of urban living—transit, lighting and communication—were well taken care of by an outburst of native mechanical genius which helped make these years the Golden Age of Invention. Some places moved forward faster than others, of course, and all lagged in some respects while advancing in others. If the rural spirit of neighborliness was submerged in the anonymity of city life, there developed in its place a spirit of impersonal social responsibility which devoted itself, with varying earnestness and success, to questions of pure water, sewage disposal and decent housing for the poor, sometimes taking the extreme form of munici-

> pal ownership. Moreover, what the great cities felt obliged to do under the whip of necessity, smaller towns undertook in a spirit of imitation, so that the new standards affected urban life everywhere. What most impresses the historical student is the lack of unity, balance, planfulness, in the advances that were made. Urban progress was experimental, uneven, often accidental: the people were, as yet, groping in the dark. . . .[35]

The record with respect to social problems, on the other hand, was generally poor. Most American cities have not solved these problems yet.

SUGGESTED READINGS

Addams, Jane. *The Social Thought of Jane Addams.* Bobbs-Merrill, Liberal Arts Press.

Addams, Jane. *Twenty Years at Hull House.* New American Library, Signet Books.

Dulles, Foster Rhea. *A History of Recreation: America Learns to Play.* Appleton-Century-Crofts.

Glaab, Charles N., and Brown, Theodore. *A History of Urban America.* Macmillan.

Green, Constance M. *American Cities in the Growth of the Nation.* Harper & Row, Colophon Books.

Green, Constance M. *The Rise of Urban America.* Harper & Row, Colophon Books.

Handlin, Oscar. *The Children of the Uprooted.* Grosset & Dunlap, Universal Library.

Handlin, Oscar. *Newcomers.* Doubleday, Anchor Books.

Handlin, Oscar. *The Uprooted.* Grosset & Dunlap, Universal Library.

Mandelbaum, Seymour J. *Boss Tweed's New York.* John Wiley & Sons.

Osofsky, G. *Harlem: The Making of a Ghetto.* Harper & Row, Torchbooks.

Riis, Jacob A. *How the Other Half Lives.* Hill & Wang, American Century Series.

Steffens, Lincoln. *The Shame of the Cities.* Hill & Wang, American Century Series.

[35] Schlesinger, *Rise of the City*, p. 120.

The New York Historical Society

Theodore Roosevelt appears as the "Apostle of Prosperity" in this 1904 campaign poster aimed at the rural voter. During his seven and a half years as president, Roosevelt did put through a number of progressive measures which benefited both farmers and city workers.

THE PROGRESSIVES

Attempts to work changes in city governments were only part of a general reform movement that swept through the nation during the closing years of the nineteenth century, a movement that generated enough momentum to endure until World War I, when domestic problems were overshadowed by events in Europe. The reformers, who at first had no name for themselves, saw the need for many changes in the United States. They wished to restore economic opportunity and competition, primarily by ending government intervention in favor of corporations and by initiating federal intervention on behalf of those with little capital or none at all. They wanted government power used to break up trusts and other business combinations and to regulate such "public" businesses as utilities and railroads. They wanted to reform government itself, to make it more the servant of the people; they believed this could be accomplished through the direct election of senators, women's suffrage, the initiative and the referendum, the recall of elected officials, and the direct primary election. As a curb on excessive wealth, they called for a federal income tax. On behalf of labor, they advocated the eight-hour day, workmen's compensation, industrial safety laws, minimum wage laws, and legislation prohibiting child labor, regulating working conditions for women, and encouraging unionization. For the poor, reformers established settlement houses—like Jane Addams' Hull House in Chicago—where they undertook to feed and clothe immigrants when necessary, teach them good health and sanitation habits, and "Americanize" them by familiarizing them with America's ways and its language.

The progressive movement, as the wave of reform came to be called, clearly owed much to Populist doctrine. Yet progressivism was more urban-oriented, more concerned with immigrants, industrial workers, white-collar workers, and small businessmen than the agrarian movement of the 1890's was. Like the Populists, however, the progressives were essentially conservative. They believed that by restoring competition in business, by making it possible for labor to combine to protect its interests, and by making government more responsive to the voters, they were promoting traditional American values, returning the country to the state of health it had presumably enjoyed before unfettered capitalism and corrupt government had injured it. Progressives did not wish to destroy the capitalist system. They admired and upheld it. But they were convinced that only through the reforms they advocated could the system be saved.

Muckraking Journalism

In his *Rendezvous with Destiny*, Eric Goldman recalled Mr. Dooley:

> "Time was," Mr. Dooley pointed out to Mr. Hennessy over his Archey Road bar, when the magazines "was very ca'ming to the mind. Angabel an' Alfonso dashin' f'r a marriage license. Prom'nent lady authoresses makin' pomes at the moon. Now an' thin a scrap over whether Shakespear was entered in his own name or was a ringer, with the longshot players always agin' Shakespear. But no wan hurt. Th' idee ye got fr'm these here publications was that life was wan glad sweet song. . . .
>
> "But now whin I pick me fav-rite magazine off th' flure, what do I find? Ivrything has gone wrong. . . . All th' pomes by th' lady authoresses that used to begin: 'Oh, moon, how fair!' now begin: 'Oh, Ogden Armour [a meat packer], how awful!' Read th' horrible disclosures about th' way Jawn C. Higgins got th' right to build a bay-window on his barber-shop at iliven forty-two Kosciusko Avnoo, South Bennington, Arkansaw. . . . Graft ivrywhere. 'Graft in th' Insurance Companies,' 'Graft in Congress,' 'Graft be [by] an old Grafter,' 'Graft in Its Relations to th' Higher

> Life,' be Dock Eliot [president of Harvard]; 'Th' Homeeric Legend an' Graft; Its Cause an' Effect; Are They th' Same? Yes and No. . . .'
>
> "An' so it goes, Hinnissy . . . till I don't trust anny man anny more. . . . I used to be nervous about burglars, but now I'm afraid iv a night call fr'm th' prisidint iv th' First National Bank."
>
> Mr. Hennessy, having read his magazine too, thought he sniffed a revolution and Mr. Dooley had to explain further. "Th' noise ye hear is not th' first gun iv a rivolution. It's on'y th' people iv th' United States batin' a carpet." Peter Dunne, the creator of the Dooley series, was as shrewd a political commentator as the United States has ever produced, and he had his muckrakers just right. Far from being revolutionists, they were the journalistic and literary voice of progressivism, expressing its indignation at corruption which cut down opportunity and its faith that moderate reform would remedy the situation. . . .[1]

Theodore Roosevelt named them, calling up the image of the Muckraker in Bunyan's *Pilgrim's Progress*, and Lincoln Steffens did much to start the trend. Sent by his publisher, S. S. McClure of *McClure's Magazine*, to find out what was stirring in the country in 1902, Steffens struck it lucky in St. Louis. There Joseph Folk had recently been elected district attorney and, much to the dismay and alarm of many influential people, he took his duties seriously. Folk uncovered unbelievable graft and corruption in the city government and endless examples of collusion between businessmen and politicians. He gave the facts to the *McClure's* editor, and Steffens detailed the whole story in the October, 1902, issue of *McClure's*. He went on to Minneapolis, Philadelphia, Pittsburgh, and other cities, finding the same general pattern of corruption and collusion.

Steffens' articles created a sensation and sold thousands of copies of *McClure's*—and the grand era of muckraking journalism was underway, to last until at least 1909. Hun-

[1] Eric F. Goldman, *Rendezvous with Destiny: A History of Modern American Reform* (New York; Random House, Vintage Books, 1956), pp. 135–136.

dreds of thousands of magazine readers were educated in the progressive cause; in some cities, reforms were actually made. *Colliers, American Magazine, Cosmopolitan, Munsey's, Hampton's, The Independent, Everybody's*—all save one museum pieces now—were the leaders; there were many less prominent periodicals whose writers dipped their pens in muck, took out after the "interests," and spread the progressive word.

S. S. McClure in 1896 commissioned Ida Tarbell to write a history of Standard Oil. The task consumed five years' time, but the results, first published in *McClure's* in 1902, were devastating. Tarbell showed in detail how the Standard Oil monopoly had been created, how it had grown, and how it had crushed rivals and strangled competition. No one could nurse any doubts about the evil of trusts after reading Ida Tarbell.

Steffens and Tarbell were only two among the numerous muckraking journalists active during the early years of the twentieth century. And the literary attack on America's ills was not confined to magazine articles. The public was bombarded with book after book exposing the seamier side of existence in the prosperous land of Social Darwinism.

Museum of the City of New York

Tommy, a shoeshine boy photographed by Jacob Riis about 1890.

Upton Sinclair took a look at Chicago's meat-packing industry and described the wretched lives and working conditions of the immigrants who labored in it in his novel *The Jungle*. Sinclair ripped the walls off packing houses, exposing the incredibly unsanitary conditions under which meat and meat products were made ready for the nation's tables. But more importantly he was concerned about the poor lot of the masses of humanity who contributed to the fortunes of Armour, Swift, and others. The book did the workers little good, but Theodore Roosevelt read it and grew ill at Sinclair's passages about meat-packing processes. In 1906 Congress passed the Pure Drug and Food Act. *The Jungle* was not the sole cause of that legislation, but it was a great contributing factor. "I aimed at the nation's heart," Sinclair later said, "and I hit it in the stomach."

Earlier, Jacob Riis had toured the slums and tenement districts of New York City; his *How the Other Half Lives*, published in 1890, revealed the squalid conditions in which immigrants lived. In 1904 Robert Hunter, a social worker, published *Poverty*, relating in detail how ten million Americans lived as paupers. Later studies indicated that Hunter had underestimated the number. Two years after *Poverty* appeared, John Spargo in his *The Bitter Cry of the Children* showed the miserable conditions in which children labored to make clothing, artificial flowers, and other items adaptable to piece work in tenement sweatshops. Frank Norris exposed the stranglehold railroads had on California in *The Octopus*. And Ray Stannard Baker wrote *Following the Color Line*, a description of black life in Jim Crow America:

Library of Congress

Mulberry Bend, one of New York City's slum areas during the early 1900's.

> One of the questions I asked of Negroes whom I met both North and South was this:
>
> "What is your chief cause of complaint?"
>
> In the South the first answer nearly always referred to the Jim Crow cars or the Jim Crow railroad stations; after that the complaint was of political disenfranchisement, the difficulty of getting justice in the courts, the lack of good school facilities, and in some localities, the danger of actual physical violence.
>
> But in the North the first answer invariably referred to working conditions.
>
> "The Negro isn't given a fair opportunity to get employment. He is discriminated against because he is colored."
>
> Of course, as a Negro said to me, "There are always places for the colored man at the bottom." He can always get work at unskilled manual labor, or personal or domestic service. He has had that in plenty in the South. But what he seeks as he becomes educated is an opportunity for better grades of employment. He wants to rise.[2]

Two Solutions for Negroes

Blacks themselves were beginning to stir against oppression, although there were two points of view about what they should do to rid themselves of second-class citizenship. Booker T. Washington, a self-taught former slave who

[2] Quoted in Alice Gordon, *The Promise of America* (Chicago: Science Research Associates, 1970), pp. 389–390.

Booker T. Washington.

had attended Hampton Institute in Virginia and founded Tuskegee Institute in Alabama, had one solution. He believed that blacks should quietly work to improve themselves to the point where whites could not help but respect and accept them. Enter professions, learn trades, start your own farms and businesses—but above all, be patient—Washington advised. With economic improvement will come economic power and eventually political and civil and social rights. At Tuskegee, young people learned trades and business skills. Among blacks, Washington was the most revered Negro of his time. Not surprisingly, he was also well regarded among whites.

William E. B. Du Bois had another answer. Born in Greater Barrington, Massachusetts, Du Bois was sent at the age of seventeen to attend Fisk University in Tennessee. There he first learned about segregation and discrimination. Du Bois came to see the world as black and white, as oppressed and oppressors. He came to believe that integration was impossible, that whites would never accept blacks, but he also believed that Booker T. Washington's gradualism was wrong. In 1903 Du Bois, then professor of sociology at Atlanta University, published *The Souls of Black Folk*, in which he wrote:

> Mr. Washington represents in Negro thought the old attitude of adjustment and submission; but adjustment at such a peculiar time as to make his program unique. This is an age of unusual economic development, and Mr. Washington's program naturally takes an economic cast, becoming a gospel of work and money to such an extent as apparently almost completely to overshadow the higher aims of life. Moreover, this is an age when the more advanced races are coming in closer contact with the less developed races, and the race feeling is therefore intensified; and Mr. Washington's program practically accepts the alleged inferiority of the Negro races. Again, in our own land, the reaction from this sentiment of wartime has given impetus to race prejudice against Negroes, and Mr. Washington withdraws many of the high demands of Negroes as men and American citizens. . . . In the history of nearly all other races and peoples, the doctrine preached at such crises has been that manly self-respect is worth more than lands and houses, and that a people who voluntarily surrender such respect, or cease striving for it, are not worth civilizing.

The results of Washington's policy, Du Bois went on to say, were political disfranchisement, the legal creation of a distinct status of civil inferiority, and the withdrawal of funds from institutions for higher education of Negroes. Du Bois did not dispute that Washington had spoken out against injustice and lynchings. But Washington had failed to recognize that slavery and race prejudice were the causes of the Negro's position, and, Du Bois argued, while it was fine for Negroes to strive for improvement, they needed help and encouragement from people who had intelligence, money, and wisdom.

> In his failure to realize and impress this last point, Mr. Washington is especially to be criticized. His doctrine has tended to make the whites, North and South, shift the burden of the Negro problem to the Negro's shoulders and stand aside as critical and rather pessimistic spectators, when in fact the burden belongs to the nation, and the hands of none of us are clean if we bend not our energies to righting these great wrongs.
>
> . . . By every civilized and peaceful method we must strive for the rights which the world accords to men. . . .

W. E. B. Du Bois.

Historical Pictures Service, Chicago

Du Bois organized a small group of black writers, professors, and doctors to meet at Harper's Ferry, the scene of John Brown's abortive attempt to stir a slave uprising in 1859. There they adopted resolutions calling for black rights in every area of American life:

> We want full mankind suffrage, and we want it now, henceforth and forever.
>
> Second. We want discrimination in public accommodation to cease. Separation in railway and street cars, based simply on race and color, is un-American, undemocratic, and silly. . . .
>
> Third. We claim the right of freemen to walk, talk, and be with them that wish to be with us. No man has a right to choose another man's friends, and to attempt to do so is an impudent interference with the most fundamental human privilege.
>
> Fourth. We want the laws enforced against rich as well as poor; against Capitalist as well as Laborer; against white as well as black. We are not more lawless than the white race, [but] we are more often arrested, convicted and mobbed. . . . We want the Fourteenth Amendment carried out to the letter and every State disfranchised in Congress which attempts to disfranchise its rightful voters. . . .
>
> Fifth. We want our children educated. . . . And when we call for education, we mean real education. . . . We will

> fight for all time against any proposal to educate black boys and girls simply as servants and underlings, or simply for the use of other people. They have a right to know, to think, to aspire.[3]

Later, in 1909, Du Bois and other blacks joined with some whites to found an organization which in 1910 became the National Association for the Advancement of Colored People. Du Bois resigned his position at Atlanta and became NAACP director of publicity and research and editor of its magazine, *Crisis.* At the time, perhaps Du Bois' greatest contribution was to turn a number of progressives away from Booker T. Washington's gradualism and toward activist demands for more immediate social, political, and economic equality for blacks. It was to be an uphill struggle, as the history of the next fifty years would show.

The Urban League, designed to meet the problems of Negroes in the cities, was organized in 1911. The League concerned itself with helping blacks who had migrated to urban centers to find jobs and housing, and it carried on an extensive program of training in social work.

Library of Congress

A suffragette posting "Votes for Women" bills with a quotation from Abraham Lincoln: "I go for all sharing the privileges of government who assist in bearing its burdens, by no means excluding the women."

Women's Rights

Industrialization caused many changes in the lives of American women. These changes were a mixed blessing, at best. Although many women found new opportunities outside the home in the new industrialized society, they also encountered many hardships. The factory system provided jobs for large numbers of young women, but the wages were usually extremely low. And all too often women workers discovered that they had escaped the drudgery of the home for that of the sweatshop.

Whatever new and nontraditional avenues American women chose, they found discrimination everywhere. In business and industry women were paid less than men for the same work. Socially, a double standard of morality was the rule. What was acceptable behavior for men usually was

[3] Quoted in Goldman, *Rendezvous with Destiny,* pp. 139–140.

considered scandalous for women. In education, opportunities were still limited despite some important gains in this field. Legal and political discrimination were, perhaps, the most serious of all inequalities. In many states married women did not have the right to sign contracts or to own property, nor did they have the right to spend their own paychecks—only their husbands claimed such rights. And nowhere in the United States did women have the right to vote until 1890, when Wyoming became the first state to grant women political equality. This small gain in political equality was no gift, however. It was won only after a long, hard struggle by the woman's suffrage movement.

The woman's suffrage movement had its organized beginnings at a convention in Seneca Falls, New York, in 1848. The movement's political struggle intensified in the 1890's, when the American Woman's Suffrage Association, led by Lucy Stone and Julia Ward Howe, merged with the National American Woman's Suffrage Association, led by Elizabeth Cady Stanton and Susan B. Anthony. This unification resulted in a renewed effort on the part of American women to secure the right to vote. Despite these organizing successes, the prospects for victory did not seem promising. By 1898 only four states—Wyoming, Colorado, Utah, and Idaho—had granted full political rights to women. By 1914 the number of equal-suffrage states had increased to only eleven. This gradual extension of woman's suffrage was far too slow for the more militant suffragettes.

The militant suffragettes, led by Alice Paul, formed the National Woman's Party, which organized many demonstrations, including picketing the White House. While such demonstrations resulted in many arrests, the pressure on politicians increased in intensity with the growing strength of the progressive movement. But the response of the nation's political leaders was disappointing. The political parties did not directly oppose the suffrage cause, but they did refuse to support a constitutional amendment. Instead, the parties shifted the responsibility to the state legislatures.

Opposition to a constitutional amendment for woman's suffrage arose from several groups. Southern politicians, for example, fought it not only from a states' rights position but also from fear that Negroes would reassert their right to vote and somehow upset the system of political control in the South. Many progressive political leaders attempted to sidestep the issue whenever possible. Theodore Roosevelt offered little support as president and did not endorse the suffrage amendment until the election of 1912, when he was the presidential candidate for the Progressive party. Woodrow Wilson continued to consider the amendment a matter for state action until he belatedly endorsed it in 1918. Although the suffragettes accused Wilson of endorsing the amendment only because of political expediency, his endorsement was an important victory. The strongest opposition to woman's suffrage came from the liquor interests, which assumed that the adoption of the Nineteenth Amendment would lead to national prohibition. In fact, the most consistent supporters of women's right to vote came from the prohibitionist forces. The antiliquor movement correctly surmised that the suffrage victory would generate the support it needed to win a prohibition amendment.

The Nineteenth Amendment finally was ratified in time for the presidential election of 1920. In addition to this victory, other reforms involving women's rights were won during the progressive era. In education women achieved greater equality in the nation's schools, and married women acquired many legal rights formerly denied them. Significant changes also were made in marriage and divorce laws in many states. While equality of the sexes would continue to be an important social issue in the future, the progressive movement did help expand women's social, political, and legal rights. Socialist Eugene Debs made this observation regarding the issues of equality: "Man has not reached his best. He will never reach his best until he walks the upward way side by side with woman."[4]

Intellectuals

Among writers, the progressive spirit reached high into academic and intellectual circles. One representative of the intellectual group was Herbert Croly, who in 1909 published *The Promise of American Life*.

[4] *Writings and Speeches of Eugene V. Debs* (New York: Hermitage Press, 1948), p. 455.

Croly was in the progressive stream, but his ideas on how to make American life better did not include a return to a time—if indeed one ever really existed—when everyone competed freely and equally for advancement. Equal rights, Croly argued, inevitably led to inequality, for the powerful and capable always won the race and tended to perpetuate their conquests. Laws themselves, he said, discriminated for one group and against one or more others. There was no such thing as a neutral law; a law was either beneficial to the public interest or it was not. The Sherman Anti-Trust Act—passed in 1890 as a beginning in trust regulation—discriminated against big business and was of dubious value to the public good because it could deprive people of the benefits of combinations. An income tax would be equally discriminatory and wrong, for the individual desire to gain wealth worked to the public benefit. An inheritance tax, while certainly discriminatory, would on the other hand be for the general good, because it was not in the public interest to preserve fortunes larger than a certain amount.

With respect to labor, Croly pointed out that unions were not so interested in fairness and competition as they were in promoting a special interest and in seeking special opportunities. Croly was not anti-union, but he did not want anyone to overlook the fact that unions suppressed competition just as ruthlessly as business monopolies did.

Big corporations and combinations, Croly went on, had contributed much to business efficiency and they proved the value of cooperation, which in itself was a good. A tendency toward monopoly was inevitable. However, when a particular monopoly was found to be contrary to the public interest, Croly thought it should be nationalized. Until then, corporations should be left alone. And unions too, when they placed their own special interests above the public benefit, should be checked by the federal government.

Herbert Croly called the system he would like to see develop the New Nationalism. It would embody an extremely powerful federal government that would regulate unions, corporations, small businesses, agriculture—all the vital aspects of the economy—whenever the national interest called for it. Croly was asking a lot of public officials, he realized, but he believed that the promise of American life could be achieved only if officials' ideas and behavior were guided by an absolute morality and a faith in human brotherhood. Only under such a system, Croly argued, could individual efforts be turned away from promoting blatant self-interest and toward cooperative endeavors to solve the nation's problems.

There were dangers, and Croly recognized many of them. Relying on "the people," progressives ran the risk of simply having one special interest group defeat another, and special interest groups could well combine to install their own kind of tryannical and greedy rule. The New Nationalism, on the other hand, could destroy political freedom. If trusts were allowed to develop, even under controls, how could they be prevented from eventually controlling the controllers? Progressive efforts to open more economic opportunities to minority groups could lead to minority chauvinism; yet, on the other hand, Croly's brand of socialism could lead to a totalitarian state that perpetuated Anglo-Saxon, white, Protestant dominance. Though not widely read, Croly's was an influential book. It would provide, in 1912, the theme for a presidential campaign.

A persistent roadblock to any kind of social, economic, and political reform had long been the courts and the philosophy of law that had prevailed in America. Numerous laws regulating interstate commerce had been declared unconstitutional, as had an income-tax statute. Efforts to abolish child labor had been struck down by the United States Supreme Court as an interference with interstate trade. Progressives contended that the courts tenaciously defended the status quo. As Eric Goldman has written:

> Basic to the American's conception of democracy was his view of law and of the Constitution, where conservatism had scored so sweeping a triumph. Nine out of ten lawyers, Richard Ely angrily estimated, were educated in a way that made them hostile to social reform. Their minds grooved by Blackstone's fears of state intervention, their adulation fixed on the resplendent corporation attorneys,

> they nodded vigorous assent when speakers told the American Bar Association that the "duty" to stop "so-called social legislation . . . devolves primarily upon our profession." As for the Constitution, that awesome subject was beyond debate. E. J. Phelps, president of the American Bar Association, expressed the opinion widespread among lawyers when he declared that attorneys should unite in "setting their feet upon and their hands against all efforts . . . to make it [the Constitution] at all the subject of political discussion."[5]

All this was to change before the twentieth century was a decade and a half old; the Constitution was to become a subject of hot political debate. Algie M. Simons was among the first to subject American institutions to economic interpretation. In his *Social Forces in America*, published in 1903 as a pamphlet and expanded into a book eight years later, Simons viewed the whole of American history through economic eyes. Decidedly Marxian, he saw the American Revolution as part of a worldwide class struggle, and the Civil War as a bitter battle between northern industrialism and southern agarianism, a conflict having nothing to do with slavery. The Constitution, according to Simons, was simply a document reflecting the economic interests of the dominant merchant-landed class, which disliked the idea of democracy and sought to perpetuate its own rule.

J. Allen Smith followed with *The Spirit of American Government*. Smith's attack on conservative economics got him fired from Marietta College in Ohio and kept him in trouble at the University of Washington in Seattle. In his major work, published in 1907, Smith focused attention on the Constitution, arguing that while bowing in the direction of majority rule, the Constitution actually and deliberately placed many obstacles in its way. Contrary to current beliefs, said Smith, laws are not fixed by nature. They are human creations, designed to serve some human end, and American basic law—the Constitution—was designed to serve a minority of large property owners intent on pre-

[5] Goldman, *Rendezvous with Destiny*, p. 102.

serving their power and preventing the landless and small farmers from achieving control of the government. So it was too with state constitutions and municipal charters, wrote Smith. These were specifically designed to allow commercial and industrial rulers to control governments and use them for their own greedy purposes while making it difficult for the general public to pin blame on anyone for corruption.

The most powerful argument concerning the origins of American basic law—*An Economic Interpretation of the Constitution of the United States*—appeared in 1913 and was written by Charles A. Beard. Combing through dusty, long-forgotten records in the old Treasury building in Washington, Beard found evidence that the framers of the Constitution, as a class, stood to benefit handsomely from the document as it was written and that such a circumstance was far from accidental. Forty among the fifty-five Founding Fathers owned public securities. Fourteen had invested in land speculation schemes. Twenty-four had money loaned out at interest, eleven had invested in manufacturing and commerce, and fifteen had investments in slaves. No member of the Constitutional Convention could be said to have represented small landholders and farmers. The men in Philadelphia had a strong interest in a government that would pay the debts of the Continental Congress at face value and with interest, that would encourage western settlement and thus drive up the price of western lands in which many had invested, that would protect and encourage trade, and that would without question protect all forms of property including slaves. Beard concluded,

> The movement for the Constitution of the United States was originated and carried through principally by four groups of personalty interests which had been adversely affected under the Articles of Confederation: money, public securities, manufactures, and trade and shipping.
>
> The first firm steps toward the formation of the Constitution were taken by a small and active group of men immediately interested through their personal posses-

> sions in the outcome of their labors.
>
> No popular vote was taken directly or indirectly on the proposition to call the Convention which drafted the Constitution.
>
> A large propertyless mass was, under the prevailing suffrage qualifications, excluded at the outset from participating (through representatives) in the work of framing the Constitution.
>
> The members of the Philadelphia Convention . . . were, with a few exceptions, immediately, directly, and personally interested in, and desired economic advantages from, the establishment of the new system.
>
> The Constitution was essentially an economic document based upon the concept that the fundamental private rights of property are anterior to government and morally beyond the reach of popular majorities. . . .
>
> The Constitution was ratified by a vote of probably not more than one-sixth of the adult males [in the country]. . . .
>
> The leaders who supported the Constitution in the ratifying conventions represented the same economic groups as the members of the Philadelphia Convention; and in a large number of instances they were also directly and personally interested in the outcome of their efforts.
>
> In the ratification, it became manifest that the line of cleavage for and against the Constitution was between substantial personalty interests on the one hand and the small farming and debtor interests on the other.[6]

Beard did not suggest that the nation as a whole had been worse off under the Constitution than it would have been had it continued under the Articles of Confederation. But he did suggest that one economic group had benefited more than any other from the document, and that the members of the Convention had been well aware of what they were doing. His interpretation was little different from

[6] Charles A. Beard, *An Economic Interpretation of the Constitution of the United States* (New York: Macmillan Co., 1913), pp. 324–325.

Simons' and Smith's, but his book was based on considerable research and he did not draw his ideas from Marxian thought or make any special pleadings. More than four decades would pass before any historian would attempt with detailed evidence to refute Beard's thesis.

In 1913 a direct attack on motherhood and the flag could not have been more shocking than Beard's *Economic Interpretation.* He had dared question the motives of demigods who had always been revered as supreme patriots, and who had practically descended from the mountain top with the Constitution. Conservatives damned Beard roundly. Progressives, on the other hand, cheered. More than anything else, the book poked gaping holes in the notion of law as immutable holy writ. If the basic document so enshrined by Americans had been written as an instrument of service to special interests, then all laws resulted from the same impulse. If law could serve one special interest, it could serve others.

In the States

One progressive journal which reviewed Beard's *Economic Interpretation* enthusiastically was *La Follette's Magazine* in Madison, Wisconsin. The magazine had been founded by a man who for many years was foremost in progressive political ranks, Robert M. La Follette. Lincoln Steffens visited La Follette for *McClure's* in 1904, when La Follette was in his second term as governor of Wisconsin. "There is trouble in Wisconsin," wrote Steffens. "I asked a few hundred people out there to explain it, and though some of them smiled and others frowned, all gave substantially one answer: 'La Folletteism.' They blame one man."

State Historical Society of Wisconsin

La Follette campaigning for governor of Wisconsin, 1900.

A conservative Milwaukee attorney told Steffens about La Follette: "He kicks about bosses and is himself a boss. He talked against the political machine and then built up an organization that is a perfect machine."

"And an agitator?" Steffens asked.

"That's the worst of him. He's not only an orator, he's a born actor; and the way that man goes around spreading discontent is a menace to law, property, business and all

American institutions. If we don't stop him here he will go out and agitate all over the United States."[7]

The trouble in Wisconsin revolved around conservative Republican efforts to block La Follette's bid for a third-term nomination. After failing to prevent his nomination at the state convention, they walked out to hold a separate convention at which they nominated anti-La Follette candidates. La Follette won the election, however, and a third term in office.

Progressive Republican Robert M. La Follette began his political life in 1880 as district attorney for Dane County, Wisconsin. In 1890, as a maverick outside the regular Republican party, he won nomination as a candidate for Congress and served four terms in the House of Representatives. Then he aimed at the governorship.

At the time, Wisconsin was as well controlled by political bosses as any state in the Union. Lumber, railroad, and industrial interests ran the state. Earlier, in the 1870's, Wisconsin had been one of the hotbeds of Grangerism, and some legislation regulating railroads was passed, only to be thrown out by the courts. In his ten-year campaign for the governorship, La Follette concentrated on two issues—the taxation of railroads on the basis of property valuation, and the direct primary. Characteristically, he painstakingly gathered facts on railroad taxation in Wisconsin and on the extent of boss rule and its effects. He was an accomplished speaker—people would have turned out to hear him had he no text but a telephone directory. Besides taking his case to the people whenever and wherever possible, La Follette also built his own political organization, which was strong enough by 1900 to gain control of the Wisconsin Republican party and nominate him for governor. He won election that year by a 100,000-vote majority.

Election to the governorship did not end La Follette's troubles with conservatives; he needed until 1906 to com-

[7] Lincoln Steffens, "Wisconsin: A State Where the People Have Restored Representative Government," *McClure's Magazine* 23 (October 1904): 563.

plete his program. But under his leadership Wisconsin became a state of model progressivism and attracted nationwide attention. The direct primary was approved by referendum in 1904. The state got a railroad commission and increased taxes on railroads. It had an industrial commission charged with regulating health and safety conditions in factories. Thousands of government employees were placed under civil service, eliminating many opportunities for political patronage. Later, workmen's compensation laws and legislation regulating working conditions for women and children were passed. La Follette had formed a brain trust of University of Wisconsin professors for researching and writing bills, and this "Wisconsin Idea," which was continued under his progressive successors, was imitated in some other states.

Robert M. La Follette did go on to agitate all over the country, as his opponents had feared he would. In 1906 the Wisconsin legislature sent him to the United States Senate, where he continued to fight for progressive legislation and to nurse presidential ambitions.

What Wisconsin got in the way of progressive legislation many other states also acquired, along with additional measures such as the referendum, initiative, and recall. But by the time La Follette had moved to the Senate, the focus of progressivism had shifted to the national level.

An obscure and demented anarchist helped cause this shift in focus. Barely six months into his second term, President William McKinley was assassinated, thus elevating Theodore Roosevelt, who had been elected vice-president in 1900, to the presidency at the age of forty-three.

Theodore Roosevelt

Born into a wealthy and distinguished New York family, Roosevelt overcame youthful physical weakness with strenuous exercise. He graduated from Harvard and spent several years as a cowboy in the Dakotas where, early in his cowpunching career, he was overheard to say to a straying steer, "Hasten forward quickly there." Later he earned a reputation as a reformer while serving as police commissioner in New York City, in the state legislature, and as governor. Boyishly enthusiastic about every idea and scheme he adopted, bellicose, outspoken, a lover of the active life, and almost simple-minded in his belief in power and patriotism, Roosevelt disturbed a lot of people. He organized the Rough Riders at the outbreak of the Spanish-American War, led the cavalry outfit as its colonel in Cuba, thought it was a "bully" war, and returned home a national hero. He was elected governor of New York in 1898. Conservative Republicans, fearing Roosevelt's popular appeal and ambition and doubting his loyalty to sound party principles, shunted him into the uninfluential vice-presidential office in 1900, hoping that the sterility of the position would quiet him and make people forget him. Unfortunately for them, McKinley was shot and killed.

Roosevelt was a reformer, but a conservative one. He was a middle-of-the-roader, noisy, but at best only a touch to the left of center. He may not have liked bosses, but he worked with them when necessary because he recognized the need for compromise in politics. He believed in a strong presidency and did not always display a fine regard for the letter of the law or separation of powers. Roosevelt intensely wanted to get things done, but he also realized that there was political wisdom in moving slowly at times.

Following the settlement of the coal strike of 1902—in which Roosevelt had taken a strong presidential hand—the president persuaded Congress to establish the Department of Commerce and Labor in 1903. Split into two departments ten years later, the agency contained a Bureau of Corporations, which proved to be of dubious use in reducing the power of monopolies.

"Trust-busting" was the most exciting of all progressive activity on the federal level early in the twentieth century, and it had plenty of public support. The Sherman Anti-Trust Act of 1890, a relatively weak law, had been little used as an instrument to break up combinations; the Interstate Commerce Act of 1887 had proved ineffective for regulating railroads. With respect to trusts, however, Roosevelt moved cautiously. He disliked many of the effects of monopoly, but he did not equate bigness with badness, regarding some trusts as "good" and others as "bad." Roosevelt's position was not entirely unlike that taken by Herbert Croly in *The Promise of American Life*; Roosevelt, an ex-president when the book appeared in 1909, read it with great interest and had long discussions with Croly about it. Mr. Dooley described Roosevelt's position on business combinations in another way:

Bureau of Engraving and Printing

Theodore Roosevelt.

> "Th' trusts," says he, "are heejus monsthers built up by th' inlightened intherprise iv th' men that have done so much to advance progress in our beloved counthry," he says. "On wan hand I wud stamp thim undher fut; on th' other hand not so fast."[8]

Roosevelt's way of working and his personality were in direct contrast to the rigidity and the tendency to demand perfection so often displayed by Robert M. La Follette, who wrote of Roosevelt:

> He acted upon the maxim that half a loaf is better than no bread. I believe that half a loaf is fatal whenever it is accepted at the sacrifice of the basic principle sought to be attained. Half a loaf, as a rule, dulls the appetite, and destroys the keenness of interest in attaining the full loaf. A halfway measure never fairly tests the principle and may utterly discredit it. It is certain to weaken, disappoint, and dissipate public interest. . . .
>
> Repeated experiences with Roosevelt had convinced me that in critical situations his action was often in direct opposition to his utterances; that one could reckon on his doing, not the logical consistent thing to carry out a definite policy, but the expedient thing, the thing that achieves temporary success. These elements in his character were matters of constant disappointment as they revealed themselves to me.[9]

[8] Quoted in Frederick Lewis Allen, *The Great Pierpont Morgan* (New York: Harper & Row, 1956), p. 175.

[9] Robert M. La Follette, *La Follette's Autobiography* (Madison, Wis.: The Robert M. La Follette Co., 1920), pp. 388, 674.

Still, something was going to happen. J. Pierpont Morgan had been more than personally saddened at McKinley's death, for he sensed, correctly, that an era had ended. When he learned in February, 1902, that the government planned to prosecute Northern Securities Company—a holding company in which Morgan was chief financier—he hurried to Washington to discuss the action with Roosevelt. According to Frederick Lewis Allen, Morgan

> protested that Roosevelt might have shown him the courtesy of advance warning.
>
> "That is just what we did not want to do," said the President.
>
> "If we have done anything wrong," persisted Morgan, "send your man to my man and they can fix it up." (He meant the Attorney General and one of his own lawyers, presumably Stetson.)
>
> "That can't be done," said Roosevelt. To which [Attorney General] Knox added, "We don't want to fix it up, we want to stop it."
>
> Morgan wanted to know whether the President was going to attack any of his other interests, such as the Steel Corporation. "Certainly not," answered Roosevelt, "unless we find out that in any case they have done something that we regard as wrong."
>
> Morgan left, so angry that according to one of his lawyers he later sat down at his hotel and wrote to Roosevelt a long and irate letter, which he was with difficulty persuaded not to send.
>
> After Morgan's departure from the White House, President Roosevelt said to Knox, "That is a most illuminating illustration of the Wall Street point of view. Mr. Morgan could not help regarding me as a big rival operator, who either intended to ruin all his interests or else could be induced to come to an agreement to ruin none."[10]

In 1904 the United States Supreme Court upheld a lower court ruling that Northern Securities had violated the Sherman Act and must be broken up. In 1905 the

[10] Allen, *Morgan*, pp. 176–177.

Court declared the Beef Trust illegal and action was taken against sugar, fertilizer, and farm machinery combinations. In 1907 Judge Kennesaw Mountain Landis found Standard Oil guilty of taking rebates and fined the trust over $29 million, a judgment later set aside as excessive.

Trusts and combinations did not disappear, however. Many more were formed during Roosevelt's presidency than were dissolved; businessmen and corporation lawyers simply found ways to pursue their ends within the law. Roosevelt had taken some action, however, and his reputation as a "trust-buster" was not wholly undeserved. His actions against monopolies made his name anathema to many men on Wall Street and they blamed his "meddling" for the Panic of 1907.

During Roosevelt's administration Congress also passed the Elkins Act, in 1903, to regulate railroad rates. In 1906 it passed the Hepburn Act, which restricted the use of free passes on railroads—a device for winning business and legislative favors—and gave the Interstate Commerce Commission power to set maximum rates, prohibit railroads from carrying goods they had produced themselves, and to insist upon uniform accounting procedures.

Other progressive legislation passed under Roosevelt between 1902 and 1908 included conservation and land reclamation laws, the Meat Inspection Act, and the Pure Food and Drug Act.

A Gathering Political Storm

Progressivism continued under Roosevelt's hand-picked successor, William Howard Taft, but more quietly. A total of ninety proceedings against trusts were brought during Taft's four years in the White House compared to forty-four during Roosevelt's seven and a half. The biggest of all, against Standard Oil, was decided in 1911, the same year the American Tobacco Company was ordered dissolved. Under Taft the Bureau of Mines was established to oversee mineral conservation. The Mann Act, prohibiting the transportation of women across state lines for immoral purposes, was passed in 1910, and the path for the direct election of senators, as well as for a federal income tax, was cleared in 1913 by constitutional amendment.

Many progressive congressmen, however, considered their party leadership too conservative. The "insurgents," as they were called, finally combined with enough Democrats to break the power of dictatorial Speaker of the House Joseph G. "Uncle Joe" Cannon to decide what bills should come before that body. This action opened wider the rifts that had been developing in the Republican party. The action of Taft's Secretary of the Interior R. A. Ballinger, who threw open to private development previously withdrawn water sites in the West and coal lands in Alaska, did nothing for party harmony either. Nor did it help relations between Taft and his patron, Theodore Roosevelt.

"Teddy" returned from an African hunting trip in 1910, restless, unemployed at age fifty, and disenchanted with the way the man he had put in office was running the government. Characteristically, Roosevelt did not keep his views to himself. He read Herbert Croly's book, became enthusiastic about the ideas Croly presented, and at Osawatomie, Kansas, on August 31, 1910, made a speech that in effect threw his hat in the presidential ring. Concerning business regulation and the power of the federal government, he said:

> I mean not merely that I stand for fair play under the present rules of the game, but that I stand for having these rules changed so as to work for a more substantial equality of opportunity. . . . The American people are right in demanding . . . New Nationalism, without which we cannot hope to deal with new problems. The New Nationalism puts the national need before sectional or personal advantage. It is impatient of the utter confusion that results from local legislatures attempting to treat national issues as local issues. It is still more impatient of the impotence which springs from overdivision of governmental powers. . . . This New Nationalism regards the executive as the steward of the public welfare [and] rightly maintains that every man holds his property subject to the general right of the community to regulate its use to whatever degree

> the public welfare may require it. . . . Combinations in industry are the result of an imperative economic law. . . . The effort at prohibiting all combinations has substantially failed. The way out lies, not in attempting to prevent such combinations, but in completely controlling them in the interest of the public welfare.[11]

The climax came two years later at the Republican convention in Chicago, where the party refused to nominate Roosevelt and stuck with Taft. The progressives, earlier organized into the National Progressive Republican League by Robert M. La Follette (who had fought for the presidential nomination himself), walked out and held their own convention in Chicago two months later. There they nominated Roosevelt for president on the Progressive—or, as it was nicknamed, the "Bull Moose"—ticket. La Follette, whom Roosevelt had used as a stalking horse in developing his campaign for the nomination in 1912, was bitter: "Even those who urged Roosevelt's candidacy as the expedient thing," he later wrote,

> were forced to admit that he was not really Progressive; that he shifted his ground; qualified his positions; compromised important issues; that nobody knew from his record that he would be found to-morrow where he stood to-day. But they justified their course by reasoning that the Progressive movement had become so powerful that, if elected, public opinion would *compel* Roosevelt to be Progressive.[12]

The Democrats, delighted at the Republican split that greatly enhanced their chances for victory, met in Baltimore. There they nominated the scholarly Woodrow Wilson, former president of Princeton University and reform governor of New Jersey.

While Roosevelt trumpeted the New Nationalism, Wilson campaigned for the New Freedom, a new spirit and attitude in American life:

> There is one great basic fact which underlies all the questions that are discussed on the political platform at the

[11] Quoted in Goldman, *Rendezvous with Destiny,* pp. 162–163.
[12] La Follette, *Autobiography,* p. 743.

> present moment. The singular fact is that nothing is done in this country as it was done twenty years ago.
>
> We are in the presence of a new organization of society. Our life has broken away from the past. The life of America is not the life that it was twenty years ago; it is not the life that it was ten years ago. We have changed our economic conditions, absolutely, from top to bottom; and, with our economic society, the organization of our life. The old political formulas do not fit the present problems.[13]

Much of the campaign centered on what to do about business combinations. Roosevelt would allow them, but regulate them closely. Wilson, on the other hand, distinguished between large corporations and trusts:

> The development of business upon a great scale, upon a great scale of cooperation, is inevitable, and let me add, is probably desirable. But that is a very different matter from the development of trusts, because the trusts have not grown. They have been artificially created; they have been put together, not by natural processes, but by the will, the deliberate planning will of men who were more powerful than their neighbors in the business world, and who wished to make their power secure against competition. . . .
>
> American industry is not free, as once it was free; the man with only a little capital is finding it harder to get into the field, more and more impossible to compete with the big fellow. Why? Because the laws of this country do not prevent the strong from crushing the weak.[14]

As to property rights *vs.* human rights, Wilson said,

> What I am interested in is having the government of the United States more concerned about human rights than about property rights. Property is an instrument of humanity; humanity isn't an instrument of property. . . . It is time that property, as compared with humanity, should take second place, not first place.[15]

[13] Woodrow Wilson, *The New Freedom* (New York: Doubleday, 1918), p. 3.

[14] Ibid., p. 15.

[15] Ibid., pp. 274–275.

Roosevelt, in a round about way, said much the same thing:

> We cordially believe in the rights of property. We think that normally and in the long run the rights of humanity, the rights of mankind, coincide with the rights of property, and that the two sets of rights are in large part inextricably interwoven; and so we would protect property in all its rights. But we feel that if in exceptional cases there is any conflict between the rights of property and the rights of man, then we must stand for the rights of man.[16]

After all the oratorical gas had cleared, Wilson easily won the election, taking over six million popular votes and 435 electoral votes. The Bull Moose was thoroughly de-antlered; Roosevelt received just eighty-eight electoral votes. Taft carried only Utah and Vermont, sweeping up the leavings—eight electoral votes.

Woodrow Wilson.

Progressivism under Wilson

The progressive movement was nearing its end, although much important legislation was enacted by Congress during the Wilson administration. Citizens got the right to vote directly for senators, and a number of them got the privilege of paying a federal income tax. The Adamson Act established an eight-hour day for railroad employees. A Federal Reserve System was created under a Federal Reserve Board that was to regulate the nation's currency and banking practices. The Clayton Anti-Trust Act—the strongest antitrust law yet enacted—was passed in 1914. This act declared also that labor unions could not be prosecuted for violating the Sherman Act provided they pursued legitimate purposes. This was no Magna Carta for labor, however; "legitimate" was open to interpretation, and the courts usually decided against unions. Finally, Congress established the Federal Trade Commission. In August, 1914, public attention turned to European war and the many problems it posed for the United States.

Progressivism had righted a number of wrongs, but it had left others, such as the unequal treatment of Negroes, practically untouched. Despite many fulminations on Wall

[16] Theodore Roosevelt, *The New Nationalism* (New York: The Outlook Co., 1911), p. 241.

Street and in corporate board rooms, it had not harmed, or seriously curbed, big business. Many progressives, like most Americans, tended to believe that to right a wrong, stamp out an evil, or bring about change, one needed only to pass a law. Business leaders—or at least their lawyers—were not stupid. Richard Olney, the man who broke the Pullman strike two decades earlier, put the case well. Commenting on the Interstate Commerce Commission to a railroad colleague, Olney pointed out that the commission could be of great use to railroads. It could be, he said, used as

> a sort of barrier between the railroad corporations and the people and a sort of protection against hasty and crude legislation hostile to railroad interests. . . . The part of wisdom is not to destroy the Commission, but to utilize it.[17]

Which brings to mind Herbert Croly's question: who would control the controllers?

In the beginning, at least, progressivism tended to be Jeffersonian in nature, its followers wishing to lead the country back to the values and traditions that prevailed in an agricultural society. Yet the issue of Jeffersonian agrarianism *vs.* Hamiltonian industrialism had been settled in favor of the latter early in the nation's history; certainly after 1865 there could no longer be any doubt as to which way the country was tending. Eventually the essence of progressivism came to be reliance on a powerful federal government that would stand between the public interest—however it might be defined—and special interests and special privilege, refereeing and regulating for the public good.

Yet the idea that anybody could get ahead in America did not die. Progressivism appealed to a wide spectrum, but it had a special attraction for small businessmen pinched by monopolistic competition and for the growing numbers of public-service personnel, professional people, salespeople, technicians, and clerical workers—almost a new class that had been spawned by industrialism itself. As Richard Hofstadter pointed out in his Pulitzer-prize-winning *The*

[17]Quoted in Goldman, *Rendezvous with Destiny,* p. 158.

Age of Reform, between 1870 and 1910 the old middle class of entrepreneurs and independent professional men about doubled in size, as did the working class and the farming group, but the new middle class increased eight times, from 756,000 to 5,609,000 people.[18] These people too wanted to get ahead; while they tended to admire the captains of industry who had so obviously fulfilled the American dream, they resented vast corporate and monopolistic power and the tycoons' swollen wealth. Wishing to "make it" themselves, members of the new middle class generally supported progressive measures that in any way showed promise of equalizing economic opportunity for them.

The progressives had their answers to the problem of preserving the benefits of industrialization and urbanization while ridding the country of the attendant evils, and some of their measures did some good. But few people at the time realized how complex the problem really was. Early in the twentieth century, America had corporate monopolies, weak labor unions, child labor, juvenile delinquency, poverty, a race problem, slums, urban ugliness, and political bosses and machines. In the 1970's the nation had corporate monopolies, powerful labor union monopolies, the military-industrial complex, juvenile delinquency and a drug problem, poverty, a race problem, slums, urban ugliness, and political bosses and machines, as well as a number of hard questions concerning the promise of American life.

Richard Hofstadter has summed up the progressive experience as well as anyone:

> The processes of modern technology and machine industry —not to speak of the complex tasks of civic life—make organization, specialism, hierarchy, and discipline utterly necessary. The Progressives, object though they might to the many sacrifices of traditional values that the new society demanded, did not seriously propose to dismantle this society, forsake its material advantages, and return to a more primitive technology. Nor did they always make the

[18] Richard Hofstadter, *The Age of Reform: From Bryan to F.D.R.* (New York: Alfred A. Knopf, 1968), p. 215.

mistake of thinking that the revolt against organization could go on without itself developing new forms of organization. They were trying, in short, to keep the benefits of the emerging organization of life and yet to retain the scheme of individualistic values that this organization was destroying. In order to understand them sympathetically, then, it is important to think of them not as stupid or incapable men who fumbled a simple task, but as men of reasonable and often indeed of penetrating intelligence whose fate it was to attempt, with great zeal and resourcefulness, a task of immense complexity and almost hopeless difficulties.[19]

SUGGESTED READINGS

Baker, Ray Stannard. *Following the Color Line: American Negro Democracy in the Progressive Era.* Harper & Row, Torchbooks.

Beard, Charles A. *An Economic Interpretation of the Constitution of the United States.* Free Press.

Croly, Herbert. *The Promise of American Life.* Bobbs-Merrill, Liberal Arts Press.

Du Bois, W. E. B. *The Souls of Black Folk.* Fawcett World, Premier Books.

Hofstadter, Richard. *The Age of Reform: From Bryan to F.D.R.* Random House, Vintage Books.

Hunter, Robert. *Poverty: Social Conscience in the Progressive Era.* Edited by P. D. Jones. Harper & Row, Torchbooks.

La Follette, Robert M. *La Follette's Autobiography: A Personal Narrative of Political Experiences.* University of Wisconsin Press.

Norris, Frank. *The Octopus.* New American Library.

Sinclair, Upton. *The Jungle.* New American Library.

Spargo, John. *The Bitter Cry of the Children.* Quadrangle Books.

Washington, Booker T. *Up from Slavery.* Bantam.

[19] Ibid., pp. 214–215.

BIBLIOGRAPHY

Chapter One

Bellamy, Edward. *Looking Backward.* Cleveland: World Publishing Co., 1945.

Ely, Richard T. *The Labor Movement in America.* New York: Macmillan Co., 1905.

Ely, Richard T. *The Social Aspects of Christianity.* New York: Thomas Y. Crowell, 1889.

Ely, Richard T. *Studies in the Evolution of Industrial Society.* New York: Macmillan Co., 1909.

George, Henry. *Progress and Poverty.* New York: Robert Schalkenbach Foundation, 1955.

George, Henry. *Social Problems.* New York: Robert Schalkenbach Foundation, 1953.

Gladden, Washington. *The Church and Modern Life.* Boston: Houghton Mifflin, 1908.

Gladden, Washington. *Social Facts and Forces.* New York: G. P. Putnam's Sons, 1897.

Gladden, Washington. *Social Salvation.* Boston: Houghton Mifflin, 1897.

Gladden, Washington. *Tools and the Man.* Boston: Houghton Mifflin, 1893.

Hodge, Charles. *What Is Darwinism?* New York: Scribner, Armstrong & Co., 1874.

Hofstadter, Richard. *Social Darwinism in American Thought.* Boston: Beacon Press, 1965.

Keller, Albert Galloway, ed. *Earth-Hunger and Other Essays by William Graham Sumner.* New Haven, Conn.: Yale University Press, 1913.

Keller, Albert Galloway, and Davie, Maurice R., eds. *Essays of William Graham Sumner.* New Haven, Conn.: Yale University Press, 1934.

Morgan, Arthur E. *Edward Bellamy*. New York: Columbia University Press, 1944.

Rauschenbusch, Walter. *Christianity and the Social Crisis*. New York: Macmillan Co., 1911.

Rauschenbusch, Walter. *Christianizing the Social Order*. New York: Macmillan Co., 1914.

Sheldon, Charles M. *In His Steps*. New York: Grosset & Dunlap, 1935.

Smith, Adam. *The Wealth of Nations*. New York: Random House, 1937.

Ward, Lester Frank. *Glimpses of the Cosmos*. 4 vols. New York: G. P. Putnam's Sons, 1913.

Chapter Two

Adams, Charles Francis. *Chapters of Erie and Other Essays*. New York: Augustus M. Kelly, 1967.

Bailey, Thomas A. *The American Pageant: A History of the Republic*. Boston: D. C. Heath, 1956.

Bailey, Thomas A. *The American Spirit: United States History as Seen by Contemporaries*. Lexington, Mass.: D. C. Heath, 1968.

Carnegie, Andrew. *The Autobiography of Andrew Carnegie*. Boston: Houghton Mifflin, 1920.

Carnegie, Andrew. *The Gospel of Wealth and Other Timely Essays*. New York: Doubleday, Page & Co., 1906.

Corey, Lewis. *The House of Morgan*. New York: G. Howard Watt, 1930.

Degler, Carl. *Out of Our Past: The Forces That Shaped Modern America*. New York: Harper & Row, 1959.

Eisenstadt, Abraham S., ed. *American History: Recent Interpretations*. 2 vols. New York: Thomas Y. Crowell, 1961.

Grodinsky, Julius. *Jay Gould, His Business Career*. Philadelphia: University of Pennsylvania Press, 1957.

Hacker, Louis M. *The World of Andrew Carnegie: 1865–1901*. Philadelphia: J. B. Lippincott Co., 1968.

Hoyt, Edwin P. *The Goulds*. New York: Weybright & Talley, 1969.

Josephson, Matthew. *The Robber Barons: The Great*

American Capitalists. New York: Harcourt, Brace, 1934.

Kennedy, Gail, ed. *Democracy and the Gospel of Wealth.* Boston: D. C. Heath, 1949.

Moody, John. *The Masters of Capital.* New Haven, Conn.: Yale University Press, 1919.

Moody, John. *The Truth About Trusts.* New York: Moody Publishing Co., 1904.

Myers, Gustavus. *The History of the Great American Fortunes.* New York: Random House, 1936.

Nevins, Allan. *John D. Rockefeller: The Heroic Age of American Enterprise.* 2 vols. New York: Charles Scribner's Sons, 1940.

Nevins, Allan. *Study in Power: John D. Rockefeller, Industrialist and Philanthropist.* 2 vols. New York: Charles Scribner's Sons, 1953.

Noyes, Alexander Dana. *Forty Years of American Finance.* New York: G. P. Putnam's Sons, 1909.

Noyes, Alexander Dana. *The Market Place.* Boston: Little, Brown, 1938.

O'Connor, Richard. *Gould's Millions.* Garden City, N.Y.: Doubleday, 1962.

Rockefeller, John D. *Random Reminiscences of Men and Events.* New York: Doubleday, Doran & Co., 1933.

Stoddard, William O. *Men of Business.* New York: Charles Scribner's Sons, 1895.

Swanberg, W. A. *Jim Fisk: The Career of an Improbable Rascal.* New York: Charles Scribner's Sons, 1959.

Tarbell, Ida M. *The History of the Standard Oil Company.* New York: Macmillan Co., 1925.

Wasson, R. Gordon. *The Hall Carbine Affair.* New York: Pandick Press, 1948.

White, Bouch, ed. *The Book of Daniel Drew.* New York: Doubleday, Doran & Co., 1910.

Chapter Three

Beals, Carleton. *The Great Revolt and Its Leaders.* New York: Abelard-Schuman, 1968.

Bryan, William Jennings. *The Commoner Condensed.* New York: Abbey Press, 1902.

Bryan, William Jennings. *The First Battle*. Chicago: W. B. Conkey Co., 1896.

Bryan, William Jennings. *The Speeches of William Jennings Bryan*. 2 vols. New York: Funk & Wagnalls, 1909.

Buck, Solon J. *The Agrarian Crusade*. New Haven, Conn.: Yale University Press, 1920.

Burlingame, Roger. *Machines That Built America*. New York: Harcourt, Brace, 1953.

Clarke, Thomas D., and Kirwan, Albert D. *The South Since Appomattox*. New York: Oxford University Press, 1967.

Cunningham, Raymond J., ed. *The Populists in Historical Perspective*. Boston: D. C. Heath, 1968.

Destler, Chester M. *American Radicalism, 1865–1901*. Chicago: Quadrangle Books, 1966.

Gladden, Washington. "The Embattled Farmers." *The Forum* 10 (November 1890): 315–322.

Goldman, Eric F. *Rendezvous with Destiny: A History of Modern American Reform*. New York: Random House, Vintage Books, 1956.

Hicks, John D. *The Populist Revolt: A History of the Farmers' Alliance and the People's Party*. Lincoln: University of Nebraska Press, 1931.

Lloyd, Caro (Caroline A.). *Henry Demarest Lloyd*. New York: G. P. Putnam's Sons, 1912.

McCormick, Cyrus. *The Century of the Reaper*. Boston: Houghton Mifflin, 1931.

Morison, Samuel Eliot, and Commager, Henry Steele. *The Growth of the American Republic*. Vol. 2. New York: Oxford University Press, 1962.

North, Douglass C. *Growth and Welfare in the American Past: A New Economic History*. Englewood Cliffs, N. J.: Prentice-Hall, 1966.

Nugent, Walter T. *The Tolerant Populists*. Chicago: University of Chicago Press, 1963.

Pollack, Norman. *The Populist Response to Industrial America*. Cambridge: Harvard University Press, 1962.

Pollack, Norman, ed. *The Populist Mind*. Indianapolis: Bobbs-Merrill, 1967.

Rochester, Anna. *The Populist Movement in the United States*. New York: International Publishers, 1943.

Saloutos, Theodore. *Farmer Movements in the South, 1865–1933.* Lincoln: University of Nebraska Press, 1960.

Saloutos, Theodore, ed. *Populism: Reaction or Reform?* New York: Holt, Rinehart & Winston, 1968.

Watson, Thomas E. "The Negro Question in the South." *The Arena* 6 (October 1892): 540–550.

Watson, Thomas E. "The People's Party's Appeal." *The Independent* 57 (October 13, 1904): 829–832.

Watson, Thomas E. "Why I Am Still a Populist." *The American Review of Reviews* 38 (September 1908): 303–306.

Weaver, James B. "The Threefold Contention of Industry." *The Arena* 5 (March 1892): 427–435.

Woodward, C. Vann. *Origins of the New South, 1877–1913.* Baton Rouge: Louisiana State University Press, 1966.

Woodward, C. Vann. *The Strange Career of Jim Crow.* New York: Oxford University Press, 1966.

Woodward, C. Vann. *Tom Watson: Agrarian Rebel.* New York: Oxford University Press, 1963.

Woodward, C. Vann. "Tom Watson and the Negro in Agrarian Politics." *The Journal of Southern History* 4 (February 1938): 14–33.

Chapter Four

Altgeld, John Peter. *Live Questions.* Chicago: George S. Bowen & Son, 1899.

Baker, Ray Stannard. *American Chronicle.* New York: Charles Scribner's Sons, 1945.

Baker, Ray Stannard. "Organized Capital Challenges Organized Labor." *McClure's Magazine* 23 (July 1904): 279–292.

Bruere, Robert W. "The Industrial Workers of the World." *Harper's Magazine* 137 (July 1918): 250–257.

Buchanan, Joseph R. *The Story of a Labor Agitator.* New York: The Outlook Co., 1903.

Cleveland, Grover. "The Government in the Chicago Strike of 1894." *McClure's Magazine* 23 (July 1904): 227–240.

Debs, Eugene V. "The Outlook for Socialism in the United States." *International Socialist Review* 1 (September 1900): 129–135.

Debs, Eugene V. "The Western Labor Movement." *International Socialist Review* 3 (November 1902): 257–265.

Dulles, Foster Rhea. *Labor in America: A History.* New York: Thomas Y. Crowell, 1968.

Foner, Philip S. *History of the Labor Movement in the United States.* 4 vols. New York: International Publishers, 1964.

Gary, Joseph E. "The Chicago Anarchists of 1886." *The Century Magazine* 45 (April 1893): 803–837.

Gompers, Samuel. *Seventy Years of Life and Labor.* 2 vols. New York: E. P. Dutton, 1925.

Gordon, Alice. *The Promise of America.* Chicago: Science Research Associates, 1970.

Haywood, William. *Bill Haywood's Book.* New York: International Publishers, 1929.

Iman, Raymond S., and Koch, Thomas W. *Labor in American Society.* Glenview, Ill.: Scott, Foresman, 1965.

Kessler, Sidney H. "The Organization of Negroes in the Knights of Labor." *The Journal of Negro History* 37 (July 1952): 248–276.

Litwack, Leon, ed. *The American Labor Movement.* Englewood Cliffs, N. J.: Prentice-Hall, 1964.

Mandel, Bernard. "Samuel Gompers and the Negro Workers, 1886–1914." *The Journal of Negro History* 40 (January 1955): 34–60.

McNeill, George E., ed. *The Labor Movement.* New York: A. M. Bridgeman, 1886.

Parsons, George Frederic. "The Labor Question." *The Atlantic Monthly* 58 (July 1886): 97–113.

Pelling, Henry. *American Labor.* Chicago: University of Chicago Press, 1965.

Powderly, Terence V. *The Path I Trod.* New York: Columbia University Press, 1940.

Powderly, Terence V. *Thirty Years of Labor.* Columbus, Ohio: Excelsior Publishing House, 1889.

Renshaw, Patrick. *The Wobblies: The Story of Syndicalism in the United States.* Garden City, N. Y.: Doubleday, 1967.

Scott, Thomas A. "The Recent Strikes." *North American Review* 125 (September 1877): 351–362.

Spaulding, J. L. "Are We in Danger of a Revolution?" *The Forum* 1 (July 1886): 405–415.

Thompson, Fred. *The I. W. W.: Its First Fifty Years.* Chicago: Industrial Workers of the World, 1955.

Werstein, Irving. *The Great Struggle: Labor in America.* New York: Charles Scribner's Sons, 1965.

Wolff, Leon. *Lockout.* New York: Harper & Row, 1965.

Wright, Carroll D. *The Battles of Labor.* Philadelphia: George W. Jacobs, 1906.

Wright, Carroll D. *The Industrial Evolution of the United States.* New York: Flood & Vincent, 1895.

Chapter Five

Addams, Jane. *The Spirit of Youth and the City Streets.* New York: Macmillan Co., 1910.

Addams, Jane. *Twenty Years at Hull House.* New York: Macmillan Co., 1924.

Cochran, Thomas C., and Miller, William. *The Age of Enterprise.* New York: Harper & Row, Torchbooks, 1961.

Commons, John R. *Races and Immigrants in America.* New York: Macmillan Co., 1907.

Darsett, Lyle W., ed. *The Challenge of the City, 1860–1910.* Lexington, Mass.: D. C. Heath, 1968.

Dulles, Foster Rhea. *A History of Recreation: America Learns to Play.* New York: Appleton-Century-Crofts, 1965.

Franklin, John Hope. *From Slavery to Freedom: A History of Negro Americans.* New York: Alfred A. Knopf, 1969.

Glaab, Charles N., and Brown, Theodore. *A History of Urban America.* New York: Macmillan Co., 1967.

Grant, Madison. *The Passing of the Great Race.* New York: Charles Scribner's Sons, 1918.

Green, Constance M. *American Cities in the Growth of the Nation.* New York: Harper & Row, 1957.

Green, Constance M. *The Rise of Urban America.* New York: Harper & Row, 1965.

Handlin, Oscar. *The Uprooted.* New York: Grosset & Dunlap, 1951.

Haynes, George Edmund. "Conditions Among Negroes in the Cities." *Annals of the American Academy of Political and Social Sciences* 49 (September 1913): 105–119.

Jones, Samuel M. "The New Patriotism." *Municipal Affairs Magazine* 3 (March 1899): 455–461.

Lynch, Denis Tilden. *"Boss" Tweed, The Story of a Grim Generation.* New York: Boni & Liveright, 1927.

Mandelbaum, Seymour J. *Boss Tweed's New York.* New York: John Wiley & Sons, 1965.

Riis, Jacob A. *How the Other Half Lives.* New York: Hill & Wang, 1957.

Robinson, Charles Mulford. *The Improvement of Towns and Cities.* New York: G. P. Putnam's Sons, 1901.

Schlesinger, Arthur M. *The Rise of the City, 1878–1898.* New York: Macmillan Co., 1933.

Shipiro, Alan; McCrea, Charles; and Beck, Vera. *Black.* Chicago: Science Research Associates, 1970.

Shipiro, Alan; McCrea, Charles; and Beck, Vera. *Growth.* Chicago: Science Research Associates, 1970.

Steffens, Lincoln. *The Shame of the Cities.* New York: Hill & Wang, 1957.

Steiner, Edward A. *The Immigrant Tide—Its Ebb and Flow.* New York: Fleming H. Revell, 1909.

Wakestein, Allen. *The Urbanization of America—An Historical Anthology.* Boston: Houghton Mifflin, 1970.

Walker, Francis A. "Immigration and Degradation." *The Forum* 11 (November 1891): 634–644.

Walker, Robert H. *Everyday Life in the Age of Enterprise.* New York: G. P. Putnam's Sons, 1967.

White, Andrew D. "The Government of American Cities." *The Forum* 10 (December 1890): 357–372.

Chapter Six

Allen, Frederick Lewis. *The Great Pierpont Morgan.* New York: Harper & Row, 1956.

Beard, Charles A. *An Economic Interpretation of the Constitution of the United States.* New York: Macmillan Co., 1913.

Croly, Herbert. *The Promise of American Life.* New York: Macmillan Co., 1909.

Gabriel, Ralph Henry. *The Course of American Democratic Thought.* New York: Ronald Press, 1956.

Goldman, Eric F. *Rendezvous with Destiny: A History of Modern American Reform.* Random House, Vintage Books, 1956.

Gordon, Alice. *The Promise of America.* Chicago: Science Research Associates, 1970.

Grantham, Dewey W., Jr. "The Progressive Era and the Reform Tradition." *Mid-America* 46 (October 1964): 227–251.

Grantham, Dewey W., Jr. "Theodore Roosevelt in American Historical Writing." *Mid-America* 43 (January 1961): 3–35.

Hofstadter, Richard. *The Age of Reform: From Bryan to F.D.R.* New York: Alfred A. Knopf, 1968.

La Follette, Robert M. *La Follette's Autobiography.* Madison, Wis.: The Robert M. La Follette Co., 1920.

Link, Arthur S. *American Epoch: A History of the United States Since the 1890's.* New York: Alfred A. Knopf, 1965.

Roosevelt, Theodore. *The New Nationalism.* New York: The Outlook Co., 1911.

Smith, J. Allen. *The Spirit of American Government.* New York: Macmillan Co., 1919.

Steffens, Lincoln. "Wisconsin: A State Where the People Have Restored Representative Government." *McClure's Magazine* 23 (October 1904): 563-572.

Watson, Richard L., Jr. "Woodrow Wilson and His Interpreters, 1947–1957." *The Mississippi Valley Historical Review* 44 (1957–1958): 207–236.

Weyl, Walter E. *The New Democracy.* New York: Harper & Row, 1964.

Wilson, Woodrow. *The New Freedom.* New York: Doubleday, 1918.

INDEX